PENGUIN B
THE PENGUIN BOOK OF MODER

D.C.R.A. Goonetilleke was born in 19
in the suburb of Nugegoda where he s
College, Colombo, and read English
Choosing to embark on an academic ca
the University of Lancaster, U.K., and is now Senior Professor of
English in the University of Kelaniya, Sri Lanka. He has been a
Visiting Scholar in the Faculty of English at the University of
Cambridge as well as a Fellow Commoner of Churchill College. He
has also held the Foundation Visiting Fellowship of Clare Hall,
Cambridge, and has been awarded the Henry Charles Champman
Visiting Fellowship by the Institute of Commonwealth Studies,
University of London. He is the Chairman of the Association for
Commonwealth Literature and Language Studies (ACLALS) and
the Vice-President of the International Association for Modern
Languages and Literatures (FILLM). His books include three
published by Macmillan (London): *Developing Countries in British
Fiction* (1977), *Images of the Raj: South Asia in the Literature of Empire*
(1988) and *Joseph Conrad: Beyond Culture and Background* (1990). He
has also edited four anthologies, *Modern Sri Lankan Stories*, *Modern
Sri Lankan Poetry*, *Modern Sri Lankan Drama* and *The Penguin New
Writing in Sri Lanka*; written a book of essays, *Between Cultures :
Essays on Literature, Language and Education*; recently edited *Joseph
Conrad : Heart of Darkness* (Peterborough, Ontario, Canada & New
York: Broadview Press, 1995); and published numerous articles in
international journals.

Professor Goonetilleke is married and has two sons.

The Penguin Book of Modern Sri Lankan Stories

Edited with an Introduction
by D.C.R.A. Goonetilleke

PENGUIN BOOKS

Penguin Books India (P) Ltd, 210 Chiranjiv Tower, 43 Nehru Place,
New Delhi-110 019, India
Penguin Books Ltd., 27 Wrights Lane, London W8 5TZ, UK
Penguin Books USA Inc., 375 Hudson Street, New York, New York 10014, USA
Penguin Books Australia Ltd., Ringwood, Victoria, Australia
Penguin Books Canada Ltd., 10 Alcorn Avenue, Suite 300, Toronto, Ontario, M4V 3B2, Canada
Penguin Books (NZ) Ltd., 182-190 Wairau Road, Auckland 10, New Zealand

First published by Penguin Books India (P) Ltd. 1996

Copyright © Penguin Books India (P) Ltd. 1996

All rights reserved

10 9 8 7 6 5 4 3 2 1

Typeset in Garamond by FOLIO, New Delhi-1

This book is sold subject to the condition that it shall not, by way of trade or otherwise, be lent, resold, hired out, or otherwise circulated without the publisher's prior written consent in any form or binding or cover other than that in which it is published and without a similar condition including this condition being imposed on the subsequent purchaser and without limiting the rights under copyright reserved above, no part of this publication may be reproduced, stored in or introduced into a retrieval system, or transmitted in any form or by any means (electronic, mechanical, photocopying, recording or otherwise), without the prior written permission of both the copyright owner and the above mentioned publisher of this book.

To my dear son Surendra

Contents

Acknowledgements ix

Introduction xi

Part One: Stories in English 1

Part Two: Stories from the Sinhalese 103

Part Three: Stories from the Tamil 177

Acknowledgements

The editor and publisher would like to thank the writers and translators whose works appear in this anthology.

The following sources are also gratefully acknowledged: Punyakante Wijenaike's 'The River' from *The Third Woman* (Colombo, 1963); Anne Ranasinghe's 'Desire' from *With Words We Write Our Lives Past Present Future* (Colombo, 1972); Chitra Fernando's 'The Chasm' from *Short Story International* (1989); Chandani Lokuge's 'A Pair of Birds' from *Phoenix I* (1990); Rehana Mohideen's 'The Wisdom Tree' and Vijita Fernando's 'Wedding in the Family' from *Phoenix II* (1991); James Goonewardene's 'The Man They Called Small-Boy' from *The Statesman* (Festival 1993); Martin Wickremasinghe's 'The Torn Coat' from *Phoenix II* (1991); Somaratne Balasuriya's 'The Cart' from *Phoenix IV* (1993).

Every effort has been made to trace all copyright-holders, but if any have been inadvertently overlooked the publishers will be pleased to make the necessary acknowledgements at the first opportunity.

Introduction

This is the first anthology of Sri Lankan stories in all the three languages of the country, Sinhalese, Tamil and English. It is a companion volume to *The Penguin New Writing in Sri Lanka*. This anthology covers a cross-section of Sri Lankan life past and present, and gives an account of the changing social fabric over a long span of history—from the heyday of British imperialism and the incursion of Eurocentric patterns of thought to decolonization and the post-colonial society with its attendant stresses caused by nationalism or class and race conflict.

It shows a more ruffled state of society than the earlier volume. Martin Wickremasinghe's 'The Torn Coat' shows the initial formality of an arranged match in the 1890s giving way to swift response and mutual attachment. At the same time, it hints at muted colonial tensions. The elite gained wealth and status by collaborating with the colonisers: so the main character, though a peasant, wants to wear a coat at his wedding, a tweed coat though he cannot pronounce the word.

The origins of prose literature in Sinhalese, however,

Introduction

go back as far as the third century B.C. when Buddhism was introduced into Sri Lanka, though the earliest extant prose works of importance date from the 13th century and were pietistic—the *Amavatura* of Gurulugomi, the *Butsarana* of Vidyachakravarti. Of special significance for the development of the short story were Dharmasena Thera's 13th-century *Saddharma Ratnavaliva* and *Saddharmalankaraya* (1398-1410) by Dharmakirthi Thera II, based on the Pali text *Rasavahini* (written in the period 1220-1295) which, in turn, was based on two earlier Pali texts *Sahassavatuppakarana* (10th century) and *Sihalavatuppakarna* (4th century), both probably based on an original in Sinhalese. The *Saddharma Ratnavaliya* and the *Saddharmalankaraya* combine an ever present moral and religious didacticism with a surprisingly rich, earthy yet subtle vein of psychological exploration dealing with the emotional impulses and social pressures that govern daily life. The *Jataka* tales (stories of the past lives of the Buddha), as used in Buddhist sermons and folk tales formed a rich oral tradition in Sinhalese.[1] But given that the vernacular story tradition—indeed, everything in indigenous culture—occupied a lowly status in colonial times, when in the early years of the 20th century W.A. Silva (1892-1957) and Martin Wickremasinghe wanted to make the short story into a literary form in Sinhalese, they also turned to European models, notably Maupassant and Chekov. 'The Torn Coat' is taken from Martin Wickremasinghe's first collection of stories, *Gehahniyak [A Woman]* (1924), written with Maupassant as an influence.

The short story in English is of more recent origin, dating from J. Vijayatunga's *Maharanee and Other Stories* (1947). It flourished after Sri Lanka's post-Independence (1948) cultural reawakening.[2] James Goonewardnene's 'The Man They Called Small-Boy' begins in the colonial days of long gowns and horse carriages, the power of the

Introduction

colonial masters and the colonial cringe, and ends with the departure of the British, leaving behind the problem of the indentured labourers they brought from India and the illicit immigrants. The main focus of the story is change of identity in relation to changes of social milieu. The chief character, Podian, an illicit immigrant, masters his fate through his adaptability and, ultimately, through spirituality. His life can be viewed in terms of 'the ancient concept, *Ganapathi,* the four ages of man: his youthful and celibate *Brahmacharya* when he learns what life has to offer him, his marital and parental *Grihastha* phase when he exercises his duties and responsibilities as householder and professional, his *Vanaprastha* or renunciation in the forest and, for a select few, the ultimate *Sannyas* of the sages.'[3] Podian is eighteen or nineteen years old when he sees and is enchanted by Colombo; so presumably his *Brahmacharya* period was in his native India. He exercises his duties and responsibilities as householder and professional as Alagu Maniampillai's major-domo. In the end, he seems to achieve 'the ultimate *Sannyas*'[4]. The salient difference between the two forms of religious retirement is that *Vanaprastha* includes the observation of ritual, while *sannyasis* go in for deeper spiritual immersion, free of ritual (meditation, trance, ecstasy and so on).

The other stories in the anthology are set in the period after Independence. Hybridity in colonial times is a concept of negative or mixed value. Marlow's fireman in Conrad's *Heart of Darkness*, a product of two cultures, appears like 'a dog in a parody of breeches' and thus signifies the degradation of the indigene. In 'The Torn Coat', the colonized collaborator goes in for mimicry and a status symbol. But in post-colonial times, hybridity is a positive or enabling concept. In Gunadasa Amarasekera's 'Going Back', the mother is educated and secure but within a single tradition; the son, benefitting from the

Introduction

increased educational opportunities available after Independence enjoys wider horizons but his hybridity is problematic too. The story portrays the unease and conflict in the mind of the young undergraduate who revisits his first home—because his book-learning and consciousness of intellectual superiority form a barrier against the spontaneous emotional ties that animate and refresh his mother, a village schoolmistress, who makes the journey with him.

Punyakante Wijenaike is an educated, Colombo based writer, yet 'The River' is a powerful peasant story with an allegorical resonance of the struggle of man with more than man, of the courage and sturdy resource that cannot outwit circumstance. Lansina Nona's final fate recalls Punchi Menika's in Leonard Woolf's *The Village in the Jungle*.

Vijita Fernando too writes in Colombo and read English as one of her subjects for her B.A. degree, yet, in 'Wedding in the Family', she is able to capture the village ambience into which she was born. The story communicates the warmth and happiness of a large extended family, very briefly assailed by a wedding and reaffirmed in the harmonious and unifying activities centred on the death of a matriarch. The paradox is that the wedding is sad while the funeral is happy.

The writers in English are able to transcend their English affiliations. Punyakante Wijenaike and Vijita Fernando are not alone. Rehana Mohideen belonged to an affluent, sophisticated, Muslim background, yet 'The Wisdom Tree', which tells of a truant who glimpses good and evil from a tree, depicts Sinhalese slum life with unsentimental warmth, humour and deep understanding. Anne Ranasinghe is a German Jew who married a Sinhalese Professor when she was a refugee in Britain, and has lived for long in the most exclusive residential area of Colombo, yet in 'Desire' she enters into the mind

Introduction

of a Sri Lankan fisherman, thwarted sexually by the wife he shares with his brother, who channels his irritation into desire for a white tourist. Capturing cross-cultural interaction, the story is psychologically coherent and telling in its detail.

Ediriwira Sarachchandra is the doyen of Sinhalese letters, having succeeded Martin Wickremasinghe. In fact, he is the country's leading novelist in both Sinhalese and English, and possesses a rich and diverse background. It is impossible to categorize him. 'Sarana' was written before he began as a novelist in English, yet his personality is already extraordinary. Illusion is seen both as a destructive and protective force when a Burgher dilettante, a would-be connoisseur of Sinhalese traditional art invests his cook with a new image, that of a dancer, an exercise which leads to near-tragedy, until Sarana creates a new, and powerful, image for himself.

Post-Independence social changes, economic difficulties and the lure of greener pastures led to migration. 'The Chasm' focuses on this now important category, the migrants—written by Chitra Fernando, herself one of them. This satire, searching rather than searing, probes the insecurities and snobbery behind the bonhomous facade maintained by a seemingly united phalanx of Sri Lankan emigres drawn from all communities, who find the certain certainties of their social status in their homeland undermined by the melting pot of Sydney. Where 'Manel, a common or garden weed' can flourish and command the respect and love of the natives, though she buds from no family tree. The chasm which provides an elemental setting elicits the elemental feelings deep within the characters, is symbolic of the elemental and also of the divisions, social and ethnic. The Sri Lankan imbroglio too appears in microcosm under alien skies.

Before Independence, national leaders, both Sinhalese

Introduction

and Tamil, were united in the struggle for freedom against the common enemy, the British. After Independence, tension arose between the communities mainly as a result of the classic colonial policy of divide and rule, privileging the minority Tamils in order to contain the majority Sinhalese. The most recent census, carried out in 1981, gave the population of Sri Lanka as over 15 million, comprising 73.98 percent Sinhalese, 12.6 percent Tamils, 7.12 percent Moors, 5.56 percent Indian Tamils, 0.29 percent Malays, 0.26 percent Burghers (descendants of the Portuguese and Dutch), and 0.20 percent others. Of the Tamils, less than half live in the North and East, that is, less than 6 percent of the population; the majority live among the Sinhalese.

'A Pair of Birds' reflects the post-colonial pressures and the estrangement of communities. Resentment and rapprochement between two young men with a long-standing friendship uncovers the uncomfortable realities and tangled complexities of ethnic conflict.

In 1988-90, in the South an insurgency mounted by the Janatha Vimukthi Peramuna (People's Liberation Front) emerged. Somaratne Balasuriya's 'The Cart' reflects the atmosphere behind it and the conditions on the ground, a portrayal of the thwarted aspirations and frustration in a developing country which breeds the violence of revolution, and the brutal violence begotten by revolution. The story has no villains, only victims. Its sheer restraint makes it both acute and moving.

The heightened style of Gamini Akmeemana's 'The Drummer' mirrors the nightmare chaos of the same period when the Janatha Vimukthi Peramuna induced a state of fear psychosis with the aim of exacting total obedience from a paralyzed population. Irrational commands were imposed on whole villages or sections of towns—to display flags at every house or go through the night without switching on a light; those who disobeyed, suffered. The seemingly surrealistic atmosphere of the story deftly captures the incredible reality. The JVP of 1988-90 was very different from the idealistic, even chivalrous JVP of the 1971 abortive insurrection.[5]

The stories in Tamil present a wide range of ordinary Tamil life. Shanmugam Sivalingam's 'Release' refreshingly reveals the balance between the daily drudgery of gaining a livelihood and a deep satisfaction life offers through connubial pleasure, sexuality and creative work, and the secret well-springs of that satisfaction. A. Santhan's 'Black Magic and Nostalgia' is a story of school-children attempting to keep a strict master away from school and their reactions and remorse when the spell—apparently—succeeds. The simple diction and directness of style lend a freshness which captures the note of childhood and its own very special modes of thought. 'Night Bird' conveys the experiences of the eight year old 'protector' of a prostitute; the bitterness of the content is in no way negated by a limpid matter-of-fact style. N.S.M. Ramaiah's 'A Basket of Shoots' is set neither in Jaffna nor in Colombo but in the plantations in the hill country, depicting the hard economic life of the descendants of the indentured Indian labourers and the romance found there.

In this anthology, there are no stories directly about the war in the North and the East because there is more than enough in the media, slanted or otherwise, and because it is impossible to give a balanced picture of the actual conflict in all its complexities.

I wish to thank Professor S. Thilainathan, Professor of Tamil, University of Peradeniya, and Mr. P. Thambirajah, Librarian, International Centre for Ethnic Studies, Colombo, for supplying me with stories in Tamil; and Dr. Lakshmi de Silva.

D.C.R.A. Goonetilleke

Kelaniya, Sri Lanka
January 1996

Introduction

Notes

1. See 'Introduction', *The Penguin New Writing in Sri Lanka* (New Delhi: Penguin Books, 1992 p. xviii.

2. Ibid., pp. ix-xi.

3. Shashi Tharoor, *The Great Indian Novel* (New Delhi: Penguin Books, 1990 edn) p. 305.

4. Ibid., p. 423, 'Glossary'.

5. See D.C.R.A. Goonetilleke, 'The 1971 Insurgency in Sri Lankan Literature in English', in *Modern Fiction Studies*, Vol. 39, No. 1, 1993; C.A. Also Chandraprema, *Sri Lanka: The Years of Terror, The JVP Insurrection 1987-1989* (Colombo: Lake House Bookshop, 1991).

Part One:
Stories in English

CONTENTS

The River Punyakante Wijenaike (1963)	5
Desire Anne Ranasinghe (1972)	14
The Drummer Gamini Akmeemana (1988)	26
The Chasm Chitra Fernando (1989)	36
A Pair of Birds Chandani Lokuge (1990)	53
The Wisdom Tree Rehana Mohideen (1991)	63
Wedding in the Family Vijita Fernando (1991)	72
The Man They Called Small-Boy James Goonewardene (1993)	79

THE RIVER

If you climb the very highest of the hills and look down you will see the river easily, far, far away at the very bottom of the valley. Twisting and turning among the trees, at first you will mistake it for a road or a cart-track or even just an empty stretch of brown earth. You will never guess its depth nor its strength because it looks wide and shallow, so calm and peaceful, like the valley itself. On a fine day you may even see little brown specks here and there and wonder what they could be. These are the boats that sail on the river when it is calm and quiet. But alas, the river is not often calm and quiet. Though one cannot believe it, this is evident in the silence that lies over the valley and in the broken crushed walls of what once used to be a proud and prosperous village. But of course you will not see this side of the river from that height. To see it in its proper light, to look beneath its flat smooth deceiving face, one has to climb down into the valley.

And to get down to the river is not easy either. First

there is the jungle, dark and misty, where the hungry leopard lurks, always in search of meat. Then there are the slimy rocks, their smooth black surfaces hiding death. And under the thorny undergrowth wait snakes and leeches, ever ready for the warm comfort of a human foot. But battle through these difficulties and the reward seems good. Gradually the jungle loses its hold on the hillside and finally gives way altogether to the rich low land bordering the river. Here nature deceives your eye, closing it to the dangers within the river. Very quickly, very cleverly she has repaired the damage of the last flood. Once more the stately coconut tree bears fruit, and its neighbour, the buxom jak fruit tree, is heavily loaded. The scent of a ripe mango, the thick rich grass, beckon man and fill him with a false promise of security. But man cannot be deceived for long. The valley is empty of all life except for one solitary hut which stands undaunted and unafraid in spite of the truth. This is the home of Lansina Nona.

*

When the river overran the village for the second time the villagers decided to move on to a safer place. They left behind them their shattered homes and ruined crops, their unrecovered dead. All that were left alive went except for Lansina Nona. She alone refused to be defeated by the river. The valley is too rich to be deserted, she said. It was her home. It had been so ever since the day she was born. She would allow no river to drive her away. She would live alone if necessary, and prove that there yet remained ways and means of outwitting the old devil.

*

When the hut was destroyed she lived on the few coconuts that were left on the trees and on a wild yam or two that she dug up from the hillside. When the water subsided, she took her hoe and walked tirelessly up and down the hill searching for a bit of land that would be safe from the river. Finally she found it behind a rock-cave, very near the jungle; the land was more or less flat there and she only had to break up the mud-clotted soil and then level and smooth it down with a rake. Then she brought out the seeds she had hoarded and saved, and scattered them over the land. She would have to wait a while yet before the taste of rice was once again in her mouth, but she did not mind how long she waited as long as she proved that life still went on in spite of the river.

Behind the rice, a little higher on the slope, she planted a bed of vegetables. Bottle gourd, a few sweet potatoes, a handful of chilli plants. Then she brought sticks and branches from the edge of the jungle and built a low fence round the whole plot.

When the boats went by on the river carrying men through the valley to the other side, Lansina Nona squatted on the bank and watched them go. Sometimes the men, curious to see this lone woman in the wilderness, drew their boats close to the land and spoke to her. There was something cheery and indefatigable in her round plump face. They had never seen such a woman before. Her eyes were the same colour as the smoke from a wood-fire and her skin was light in colour. It was not the golden fairness of the hill country women but a strange pale colour like milk which had been treated with water. She told them that her father had been a white man who had passed through the village long ago. That was why her mother had named her Lansina Nona, meaning half-white.

From the men she learned bits of gossip about what went on in the outside world and in return she entertained them with stories of her own making. Once she even got them to bring her a goat so that she could give them milk when they were thirsty. But never once did she touch on the hardship she endured and of the ever-present danger hiding beneath the river. One by one the men kept on trying to persuade her to come with them.

'Now what is the use of staying here alone? Come with us, *Akke,* and we will find you a good place to live in. Round that hill now there is a good village and the people are friendly. There the river runs too low for it to rise up and flood the land and the soil too is good and fertile.' But she remained stubborn.

'I was born here and I will die here when the time comes' she said. 'But when I die it will not be through drowning. Of illness, of old age, who knows? We have to die some day. Maybe the leopard that is said to live up in the jungle will come down and kill me. What is the use of running here and there *Aiya?* Besides I am not afraid of the river. I will not let it drive me away from here.'

'But it is dangerous and foolish to shut one's eyes to the river. What chance will you have against it alone?'

Lansina Nona smiled.

'Do not worry, *Aiya,* the river cannot hurt me. I have grown wise and cunning with the years. See this time the rice is planted where the river cannot go. And when my hut falls I will climb to that cave up there on the hill and live. There are ways, *Aiya,* there are ways of living if one wants to, in spite of the river.'

*

A month later the rains started. Lansina Nona awoke to the pattering of it on her roof. She went to the door and looked at the river. It lay still except for the movement of the rain beating down on it. Lansina Nona was glad that the rains had come early, in time to water her rice. It stood six inches high now and each morning she would climb up and look at it proudly. Yes, let it rain, till the rice was well-watered and after that let it stop. She scanned the sky carefully. The clouds were light, the rain would not last very long. She went inside and as there was nothing else to do, she took her black *bana potha* and sat down to read. This was the only book she had read in her life, other than her old school books. Its pages were worn out and sometimes torn and she knew practically every word by heart, but still she read it. Not because she was interested or because she was religious minded but simply out of habit and partly because she could never sit still without doing something.

Though by nature she was not one of those women who spend their lives worshipping at some shrine or other, still, she was scrupulous and methodical about her daily devotions. The habit had been ingrained in her ever since she stood as a toddler at her mother's knee. An old Bo-tree which had withstood the flood, served as her worshipping place. She nailed a small box to its trunk and inside this she placed a small broken headless statue of the Buddha. Across it she strung a bit of coloured cloth like a curtain and an oil lamp, always lit, was placed beside the statue. There was no incense to light and no flowers to offer but the headless image did not seem to mind. She had found it lying half-buried in the mud near the river.

The rain did not cease as she had anticipated. It kept on and on and soon the river began to rise again, little by little. Rarely did a boat go by now and when it did the boatman would shout out urgently:

'Come, *Akke*, come. Aiyo, what foolishness is this? See the river is rising. Everyday it is rising'

But she only smiled and waved them on.

'Do not fear, *Aiya*, do not fear. Do I not know the river like the palm of my hand?'

One morning when she opened the door of her hut she found the water moving around like a thief trying to find a way in. Then she took the goat and whatever she could carry, and went up the hill to the cave. Half-way up she stopped and looked down. The water had entered the hut. Now she could not go back even if she wanted to. But she had everything she wanted in her hands, so there was no need to go back. Her mat, her cooking pot, a lamp and the book.

Before the rice could spoil from too much rain, she took her hoe which she had kept hidden in the cave and cut small neat grooves round the sides of the field and let some of the water run out. Earlier she had stored a supply of coconuts and vegetables in the cave. Now she lived on these and laughed at the river.

'So you thought you would get me this time did you?' she shouted out merrily. 'Well, see if you can rise even as high as that tree over there before you make me worry.'

As if resenting her arrogance, overnight the river turned angry. The water lashed with fury against the trees breaking them in two and Lansina Nona's hut was uprooted from its foundation and torn to pieces. The rain increased its strength and the wind howled dismally round the valley. At last even Lansina Nona had to admit the strength of her enemy. Like a king it rode, carrying everything in its power and showing no mercy on anything that opposed it. From her high perch she saw the dead bodies of dogs and cattle rush by.

'By staying on I have saved my life,' thought Lansina Nona. 'This time the river has gone beyond the valley and destroyed other villages. Aiyo, aiyo, how foolish it is to run away. By running they have not escaped.'

*

But at last the rain ceased. Lansina Nona had thought she would never see the sun again but when she awoke that day, there it was as big and powerful as ever. And it was wondrous how the sun could change everything. The bedraggled trees lifted up their heads with hope and the birds came out to sing and dry their dampness. Even the destruction did not seem so heavy under the sun. But the river did not leave the land easily. It clung on with a relentless unyielding hold and its face smooth and still again, gave no sign of the evil undercurrent beneath. An evil so great that it carried disease and death at the same time as it quietly sucked the good earth and drank the life blood of the land.

Lansina Nona looked about her sadly. It would take many months before the land recovered again from its loss. Her shrine box was broken and the little headless image had gone back to the river. But she herself was alive and whole and the rice was safe on the hillside. This at least she had proved. The river had been unable to reach her.

But two days later her store of food was finished and there was nothing to eat in the cave. The day before she had noticed some wild berries growing higher up on the hill near the jungle. She looked about for a long stick to the end of which she tied her rake. Armed with this she ventured up the steep climb to gather them. The higher she went, the bigger the fruit and soon she found herself entering the jungle.

'Cut down the jungle and many can live here safe from the river,' she thought.

Then she discovered the rock, big and strong, rising out from the side of the hill. It struck out many feet away from the hill and was broad and flat and easy to walk on. On it there was nothing but a few windblown tufts of grass growing here and there and as she walked across she could feel the rock heating up under the sun.

But at the end of the rock the drop down to the valley was terrifying. Never had Lansina Nona seen anything like it before. She felt dizzy and faint and stepped back hurriedly. Why, from here the whole valley could be taken in at one glance! And also the whole terrifying scene of destruction. The valley was nothing but a sheet of water carrying upon it the stillness of death. No life of any sort except for a few hawks that circled round and round screaming hungrily. Here on the rock she felt that out of the whole world she was the only person left alive.

She felt dazed. Never had she imagined that the river held such vast power to destroy. Then her heart began to beat with thankfulness that she had been saved and also with a strange new sense of power. Yes, she alone had been left alive to prove her courage and wisdom. Now they would all listen to her when she told them to come back again to the valley. To come back to a new life here on the hill.

'Up here it is quite safe' she would say. 'And from this rock here one can sit and watch the land below getting flooded without even wetting one's feet. And there is nobody here to fight and say that the jungle belongs to him. All this rich land waiting for the one with the most courage to come and take it.'

Then suddenly she became aware that she had made a mistake in believing that the jungle was empty. She became aware of the presence of another there, just behind the rock, under the trees. A shadow moved, a leaf rustled.

'It is a bird or a monkey,' she said loudly. 'Though it is too windy up here for any creature so small.'

Then a yellow head peered above the rock, followed rapidly by a yellow form streaking across the rock. Brought face to face, the woman and the leopard halted confusedly within a few paces of each other. Then slowly the leopard retreated a few steps and stopped. Lansina Nona's mouth dropped open and she began to pant, softly at first, then louder and louder till the panting became the only sound in her ears. The leopard glared balefully at her, then took a hesitant step forward. Lansina Nona's eyes protruded out of her head and rolled hither and thither like loose pebbles. She was unaware of her body moving slowly backwards. To the leopard's one step, she took two, though she did not know it. On and on the two moved across the surface of the rock and then Lansina Nona felt her foot touch nothing but the empty air. Her body jerked backwards and with a twist she fell off into thin air. She was conscious of the wind roaring in her ears and then she saw the river come rushing up to greet her. Closer and closer came the river, its face smooth and smiling in triumph. Then at last her mouth opened and gave a scream so piercing in its agony that it echoed round and round the valley long after she was gone. And some say that to this day it can still be heard, if one cares to listen, whenever the river floods the valley.

DESIRE

In that heavy hour after the midday meal the beach lay deserted under a fierce tropical sun. But some fishermen sat playing cards in the shade of a row of catamarans drawn up high on the dunes against the tide. Their bodies were corded and hard, burnt black by continual exposure. Their huts—temporary, for with the changing monsoon they migrated to the other side of the island—were placed higher still. Some mechanized fishing boats were gently riding at sea; they looked very gay, painted red and yellow, white and blue.

Ravi too had been gambling, but luck was against him and he had lost his last two rupees. He was young, with a shock of thick black hair sleek with coconut oil, and cheek-bones that projected high and sharp beneath a pair of quick shifting eyes. Ravi had a special problem. He lived with his brother Joseph, and they shared a wife. Padma was still a girl, with provocative breasts and hips that swayed invitingly when she walked barefoot over the sand . . . . Ravi stirred at the thought of her. But inexplicably she had become cool towards him, feigning tiredness and sickness, even disappearing from their hut on the nights that his brother went fishing and the marital rights fell upon him.

That was the reason for Ravi's gambling to-day. He had calculated that if he were to buy her a present—a couple of yards of bright cloth maybe, or some coloured glass bangles, she might change her mind in his favour. And now even that chance was gone. Dully he leant against the boat. Another lonely night, unless he forced her. But he rejected the thought. There'd be no pleasure, and life afterwards would be impossible with her.

He jumped up, throwing down his cards. He might as well go and see to the nets.

It was then that he saw two European women wandering along the beach. He stood, fascinated. That one with the yellow hair. How could this shameless girl walk around like that? But she was lovely, there was no doubt. Ravi watched with increasing interest as they came closer. He shouted to the other fishermen: 'Hey, look at this, what's coming!', and they all guffawed raucously. It was unheard of for women to move about like this, alone, but then these foreigners, there was no accounting for what they do . . . .

They were an oddly assorted pair. The older of the two was at least fifty, possibly more. Plump and short, she sported an elegant straw hat from which a few wisps of gauzy decoration floated. Her flowered silk dress fitted tightly over an ample bosom. She wore white gloves, and her stockinged feet were encased in high-heeled shoes which made progress in the sand precarious. The younger one could not have been more than eighteen. Her sleeveless and low-cut frock was very short, exposing a tantalizing pair of slim brown legs. In one hand she was carrying her sandals. Both women kept their eyes on the sand because they were collecting shells which the older one assiduously popped into a large, expensive looking handbag.

Sonia, the young girl, was on her way to Australia where her fiance was waiting for her. She glanced up and saw the fishermen. Gaily she returned their stares, she was used to male admiration, and their looks did not disconcert her in the least. On the contrary. She felt complimented by them. It did not occur to her for a moment that here, in the East, in this far-off place, attitudes might be different. Her eye met Ravi's, he was standing apart from the others, and he smiled at her. She smiled back. And in that moment Ravi had an idea. He shouted to the girl.

'Lady like ride in boat?' and when she did not at once reply, 'I know place where plenty shells . . . BIG shells . . . . ' His hands indicated the size of the shells.

The girl shook her hair back and laughed. 'Where?' she shouted back.

Ravi ran over to where the women were standing. He tightened his sarong, then pointed to the far side of the bay where it curved into a rocky projection. 'Past there'. He fumbled for words, his English was limited, picked up during the occupation of the British in the neighbouring harbour.

'Past rock . . . lovely shells. Place called Marble Bay.' He became more enthusiastic as the idea took hold. 'Lady go in boat. Lady pay little money . . . I take lady!'

Sonia looked at her companion. Mrs Lydia Harbottle was the widow of an American industrialist. They had met en route, and as they were both alone and both considered themselves rather adventurous, they had joined forces. It was really Mrs Harbottle who was keen on rare shells.

Desire

'What d'you say, Lydia? It would be fun, wouldn't it, and make a change?'

'I couldn't go in one of those, my dear.' Mrs Harbottle shook her head emphatically at the fragile catamarans. But Ravi had anticipated her.

'Lady go in motorboat . . . . ' He nodded at the painted ones, sitting so sweetly on the flat, shining sea. 'Quite safe. I take lady,' and giving a self-satisfied smirk which showed his betel-reddened teeth, added 'I very good in boat!'

He laughed happily. This would settle his troubles. He could easily handle the small craft alone, it merely meant crossing from one bay to the next. True, of course, one had to know the currents. But Ravi had plenty of experience and was quite familiar with these waters. He moved closer to the young woman. He saw that her eyes were grey and had little flecks of colour in them. 'We go?' he asked again.

Lydia Harbottle was not sure. Had she been alone she would never have considered the proposition. But now she was torn between her elderly sense of carefulness and the attitude of daring she affected to hide her age from herself and to impress Sonia with her youthfulness. She did not want to let herself down in front of Sonia. She looked at the sea. But there was no excuse there—it lay absolutely calm in the afternoon sun, a deep blue under a paler sky. 'What do you think, Sonia?' she said uncertainly.

'Oh, I would love it.' The girl again shook her hair back. 'Let's find out what this chap wants for taking us.' She turned to Ravi. 'How much?' she asked.

Ravi quickly debated with himself. If he asked too much they might not go at all. On the other hand, they looked rich. He had noticed the magnificent sapphires in Mrs Harbottle's ears. And she had not even pierced her ear-lobes like the local women—what a risk

17

to take, the ear-rings were held in place only by tiny screws.

He said, 'Ten rupees,' and took a deep breath.

Sonia giggled. 'Alright,' she said.

When he realized he could have asked for more he added hastily, 'And diesel oil . . . for engine . . . .'

She nodded. With a small whoop he ran into the sea and swam out to the boat.

It was now extremely hot. There was an almost ominous sultriness in the air, but the two women being foreigners would not have realized it. Mrs Harbottle did not want to disagree with dear Sonia, but somehow, deep inside, she felt she should not be going. A little timidly she asked, 'Do you really think it will be alright, my dear?' but Sonia was already running out to the red-painted boat that Ravi was skilfully manoeuvring towards the shore. She was up to her knees in water, Ravi held out his hand, and without hesitating she allowed him to help her into the boat.

Ravi had never seen a white woman from so near, and he had certainly never touched one. He felt intoxicated with the turn of events and his luck, with the sight of the girl, her smooth tanned skin and those legs . . . he could not take his eyes off them. The thought of the money made him feel rich. Now Padma too would cease to be a problem.

He bent down to help the older woman into the boat. She was heavy and it was not easy. Then he straightened and shouted to the fishermen who had been watching the whole performance gleefully from the shore. They roared with laughter. Ravi threw the switch, the engine started; he turned the boat smartly and headed out to sea.

Mrs Harbottle immediately felt uneasy. But Sonia was quite relaxed. Hands trailing in the water she sat and serenely watched the beach recede. And while Sonia watched the beach, Ravi watched Sonia. His thoughts were becoming confused—his desire for Padma became desire for this strange white woman. His heart was beating so fast as he stood handling the tiller that he thought he would choke. Meanwhile the older woman was talking and talking—would she never stop?—with what appeared to him to be a note of impatience in her voice. But the young one kept smiling, what a flirt she was, and replying in short sentences that did not however seem to pacify the older one.

They rounded the rocky promontory and Marble Bay lay before them. Sonia cried out at the beauty of it. Here too the water was blue but so clear that they could see the white sand at the bottom, and the shadows of fish outlined against it. The whole bay was totally deserted, and so was the sandy shore that curved in a perfect arc from the rocky protrusion right to the other end, maybe two miles away. Thick scrub jungle enclosed the bay from end to end.

Ravi brought the boat as near as he could to the beach, then dropped her anchor. Before Sonia had a chance to jump out he was beside her, ready to help her, to touch her again.

There were indeed many shells. The old lady immediately began to collect them, she needed activity to rid herself of her increasing sense of fear. Because of her shoes she decided not to venture too far, in any case, it was not necessary. Meanwhile Sonia was running along the beach, Mrs Harbottle could see her picking up shells and giving them to Ravi who was following her. She gave a sigh. Might as well make the best of it, now that they were here.

Sonia was running along the beach and Ravi watched her picking up shells, and then he too picked them up for her, and she would hand him hers to roll in the top of his sarong. His eyes never left her. When she bent down he glanced down the front of her dress, and he could see the skin where the breast divided. He felt the blood surge to his head, drumming in his ears, he saw the girl's eyes and felt drunk. With a shaking hand he pointed, 'There,' he said. 'There—the best shells of all.'

The place he was indicating was a depression in the sand where a stream left the jungle to flow into the sea. In the shallow basin, brought in by the tide, lay beautiful shells of all colours and sizes, and this miniature delta spread right back into the jungle. Skilfully he led her away from the beach. 'Elephants?' she asked.

He nodded. 'Yes', he said, 'Elephant.' He rolled the word round his mouth, happy to have understood her. 'And monkey. And snake.' He wriggled his forearm to demonstrate.

The heat was oppressive although the sun was no longer overhead. Sonia sighed and brushed her hair back from her sticky forehead. Ravi nodded again, knowingly. 'Lady tired. Lady rest . . . here.'

To reinforce his words he sat down. She too sank gratefully into the soft warm sand beside him. 'Goodness,' she muttered. 'I just didn't realize I was so terribly tired.'

Her words were meaningless to him, but it did not matter, his heart was beating madly—he only saw her grey eyes with those strange dancing flecks in them, and her legs, now on the sand, long and smooth and within reach of his hands. And he forgot everything, in a wild leap he threw himself on the girl. He felt her pointed breasts under the thin stuff of her dress against his bare chest, and before she could make a sound he put his mouth over hers, hard, while his hand slid along her legs, parting them, first gently, then as she struggled harder, more roughly; it was all he could manage to keep her pinned to the ground.

It was the wind that brought him to his senses as he lay

there exhausted, all passion spent. It came quite suddenly, from the sea, sweeping over the scrub jungle and crackling in the dry leaves. He sat up. The girl had gone, all the shells they had collected lay scattered on the ground. But he had lost interest in them. He got up. And as he reached the beach he saw the girl ahead of him, running, running towards the other woman and the boat. He felt vaguely cheated, empty inside.

Sonia was running, shouting as she was running though there was no one to hear. Her nostrils were still filled with the smell of the coconut oil on the man's hair, she felt sick at the thought of his betel-stained teeth, his probing hands and hard, inconsiderate body. God, what a fool she had been, what an utter fool!

And then she noticed that the sun was going down, it was poised just over a bank of clouds spreading rapidly from the horizon, and that the quick, early tropical dusk had begun to fall. But more than the gathering darkness in this lonely place with the rising voices of the jungle, the sea frightened her. It was no longer smooth. Pale green rollers were breaking in an avalanche of water, and all the way out there was a continuous procession of waves. She suddenly felt terrified, soiled and incredibly lonely. She longed for Mrs Harbottle. There—she could see the dark figure outlined against the sky. She ran faster, as if running could cleanse her, would erase what had happened. The jungle noises became more insistent, and now the sun disappeared completely, dropping into the sea. Immediately a greyness enshrouded everything. And then the wind blew in from the sea, a harsh gust that shook the branches of the scrub lining the beach.

Here, at last, was Mrs Harbottle. Sonia ached for motherly comfort. She called out to her as she covered the last stretch of sand that lay between them.

But Mrs Harbottle was furious. She had been worried

when the girl had disappeared and seeing her back apparently safe, her worry was replaced by an anger that contained all the accumulated tension of the long hot afternoon. As the girl came nearer she tried to control herself but her voice betrayed her. 'Where for God's sake have you been?' she said roughly. 'What d'you think you're doing, leaving me here all alone!'

The girl was panting. She looked at the angry face, at the smudged make-up and the absurd hat with its wisps of gauze, and at once she knew that there'd be no comfort. Trying to regain her breath, shaking, she stood there and then, with a half sob she said:

'I . . . I'm sorry I left you. I went to get shells for you . . . ' and then, breaking down completely, she burst out, 'Oh, you don't understand anything—that chap—God, that chap *raped* me!'

She turned and raced into the sea, towards the boat where it lay tossing in the waves.

Mrs Harbottle stood stunned, her face twisted with horror and repugnance. At that moment Ravi arrived. Mrs Harbottle's fury now burst in an uncontrolled torrent. She began to abuse and threaten him regardless of the fact that he could not understand a word she was saying, intercepting him as he tried to reach the boat. He attempted to pass her but she got hold of him, pummelling his chest with her fists, all the while screaming in a high wild voice.

He pushed her unceremoniously aside. Then waded through the water. It was almost dark. Again the wind rose from the sea, a long roar, driving the clouds before it. Mrs Harbottle ran after Ravi, stumbling through the water to the boat. Sonia leant over the side to help her, but it was not easy for the waves were tossing the small craft up and down.

Ravi took no notice of the two women. He had started the engine and was lighting a hurricane lamp which hung beside it. Then he turned and watched them struggling yet making no effort whatever towards them. Mrs Harbottle, half in and half out of the rocking boat, was frantic with fear and anger. Again she screamed at him. But he was bored with the whole expedition, he knew he had forfeited the ten rupees after what he had done to the girl.

Nor was he at all sure what these two fanatics would do next.

He loosened the oars to help him push off. In the back of his mind there was a vague fear that the old woman might even go to the police.

When ultimately he realized that Sonia would not be able to lift Mrs Harbottle into the boat without assistance he slowly made his way over to them. Dropping the oar from his left hand, casually and almost insolently he pulled the bedraggled woman up over the side.

And she, now beside herself, gave him a resounding slap.

The boat rocked. For a moment Ravi was caught by surprise. His eyes fell on Sonia who stood trying to balance, and the thought passed through his mind that she was not pretty at all. Her eyes were quite ordinary, and her hair—why, it was thin and straggly. Whatever had possessed him.

And then Mrs Harbottle gave him another slap.

His face contorted with rage. He lifted his right hand, and with the oar he still held in it he hit her, once, hard and with all his strength.

She made no sound at all. There was only the crack of the impact, and Sonia's gasp as she lunged forward to catch the woman in her fall. But Ravi was too quick for her. He pushed her away harshly. Mrs Harbottle dropped heavily, her head lolling, while blood poured from her scalp. In the dancing light of the hurricane lamp her skin looked grey, and her eyes showed white between half open lids.

Ravi's face was expressionless as he went back to the tiller. Not far ahead was the promontory, it was barely visible in the darkness. The current here ran out to sea; he had to be quick to do what he knew had to be done.

He shouted roughly at Sonia when he saw her edging towards the old lady's body. She shrank back and cowered, shivering, in the prow of the boat. She was watching the sea, and with increasing terror, Ravi's face.

And now the squall burst. Ravi seemed quite unaware of it. He bent over Mrs Harbottle where she lay, and with a swift, half furtive movement pulled off her ear-rings, tucking them into the top of his sarong where earlier he had kept the shells. The boat was tossing, and the rain was a solid slanting sheet across the sea. He lifted Mrs Harbottle's legs over the side of the boat, then, waiting for a wave to help him, with a quick powerful shove he heaved the inert body overboard.

The girl screamed sharply. But her voice was lost, dispersed by the wind. Ravi returned to the engine. He felt neither wind nor rain, all he could think of was the fortune he was carrying rolled in his sarong. Who cared about ten rupees now, why he'd be able to get a hundred times as much with these ear-rings, or even more, with luck!

And then it occurred to him that the only obstacle between him and happiness was the girl.

With the back of his hand he wiped the water of his face. He felt strong and powerful—insuperable. Without shifting his position he groped for the oar with his foot, then bent to pick it up. He lifted it, nonchalantly, as if he were about to slip it into the locks though the motor was throbbing steadily.

It took only a few seconds, and she didn't even have time to cry out.

Back on shore, the fishermen stood debating whether to take the boats out for the night's fishing in view of the high sea that was running. The rain put an end to their discussion. They were looking out for Ravi, but Joseph, Ravi's brother, reassured them. 'Don't worry about him', he said. 'He knows the sea. He'll look after himself and the boat.'

They were easily persuaded, for the rain was coming down hard and they were keen to get back to their huts. They hung a lamp from the mast of one of the beached catamarans, to guide Ravi in.

Joseph had been right for not much later Ravi anchored his boat to the buoy. When he saw the lamp through the rain he smiled to himself—they had remembered him then! He placed the two ear-rings in his mouth, and tucking up his sarong, jumped into the sea. He swam ashore, and once safely there spat the ear-rings into his hands. Holding them carefully he sprinted up to where the lamp was swinging on the catamaran, where he had lost at cards only this afternoon.

He raised the stones against the lamp. How richly they glowed, throwing off scintillating sparks where the sapphires had been cut, and where they refracted the light through the drops of rain. Fingering them lovingly and with infinite care he rolled them back into the top of his soaking sarong.

He had an overwhelming feeling of relief. With a light step he climbed up over the dunes, searching for his brother's hut in the rain.

The Drummer

The drumming would wake Daniel up and he would lie there on his bed, full of resentment. He habitually read till late and he was used to waking up late too; but this fellow would begin his silly drumming at six in the morning, when Daniel would have preferred to have at least another hour's sleep.

He wasn't the only one in the neighbourhood who was suffering because of the drummer. The houses jostled and crowded each other down the lane that was so narrow that two cars had trouble passing each other. All the houses had their radios, stereos and televisions, etc. and the lane had never been as quiet as Daniel would have liked it to be.

The drummer was a menace. Daniel had to admit that the variety of rhythms that the drummer practised, traditional as well as western, were excellent. But six in the morning wasn't a good time to enjoy the excellence of somebody's drumming, particularly when it jerked him mercilessly out of sleep day after day.

The Drummer

People complained to each other about it, and threatened to chase the fellow out, whoever he was. They were particularly indignant to learn that the fellow was a total outsider who had rented an annexe from Mr Silva, a respectable, second-generation resident of the lane.

Everyone complained to Mr Silva, and he told them, bleary-eyed from lack of sleep himself that there was nothing he could do. His annexe had been vacant for nearly two years. Now this fellow had taken it at last. If he was chased out, would they find him another tenant? No matter how much he was irritated by the drumming, Mr Silva wasn't going to tell the fellow to pack his bags and go. If they wanted to, they were welcome to do that themselves.

It was said that Mr Schokman, who lived next door to Mr Silva, did complain to the fellow. And it was said too, that the fellow smiled, nodded his head, and went on with his drumming as if nothing had happened.

Nothing had happened, really. All that had happened was that somebody they said it was Mr Schokman had complained. A complaint, after all, was nothing. So Daniel found himself smoking more, biting his nails, and losing his temper even with his pet cocker spaniel. And he hadn't even seen the fellow.

But Daniel's neighbour Raja one evening showed him who the fellow was. They were talking as usual, standing on either side of the croton hedge that separated their tiny gardens, when Raja suddenly fell silent and looked at a young man who was walking down the lane.

'It's him', Raja said vehemently before the fellow had gone out of earshot. It took Daniel a moment to realize that Raja was talking about the drummer.

A very ordinary, insignificant looking fellow, Daniel thought, in very ordinary clothes too; who would have thought that he was the notorious drummer. He must have heard Raja's voice, but he simply kept on walking, paying no attention.

Daniel preferred not to antagonize the fellow. Daniel was a peaceful man and he chose to live here because it was a peaceful area. Even though the music from the houses was always too loud, there were no drunken brawls and the neighbourly disputes were usually settled without any physical violence.

People gossipped and destroyed each other's reputations, but that was not at all the same thing, not as vulgar, as physical violence. Even if there were riots in the city, people listened to their stereos down the lane and life would go on as wonderfully as ever before.

The drummer had changed all this. It was true that one hardly ever saw him. But now he was drumming in the afternoons too, and it became particularly bad during the holidays. Somehow, people who lived down the lane were not the same any more. They muttered and grumbled in undertones, and fell completely silent when they occasionally saw him.

No one, not even the Silvas, knew much about the fellow; where he had come from, where he worked, what his name was. All they seemed to know was that he drummed incessantly.

Sometimes he wouldn't be there at all for days. Or rather, he didn't drum. The silence then became uncanny. They couldn't really get used to it. The silence got on people's nerves, as much as the noise of the drumming did.

And then, just as people were beginning to get used to the eerie silence, the fellow would begin his awful noise again. It shattered their nerves. People went about bleary-eyed, lost their temper for nothing, and cursed the drummer in barely audible undertones.

There were some, particularly those with a grudge against the Silvas, who said they were actually happy with the drumming. It was a change, they said, from the monotonous stereos. But they suffered from the drumming as much as everybody else did.

And no one even complained any more; at any rate, not directly to the drummer. It was said the people who had complained to the drummer about the noise had received letters which said, simply: 'Pay attention!' The letters were anonymous, but it was assumed that they referred to the drummer.

Not that there had been any hint of physical violence on anybody's part. But there was a fear, never openly admitted, that prevented anyone from throwing a stone at the fellow's window in the dark. Daniel, who disliked the idea of a situation deteriorating into physical violence, wouldn't have approved of such lawlessness, in any case.

Not that anyone had talked of violence. But Daniel sensed this air of menace. People switched off their radios, hi-fi sets and televisions when the drummer began his noise. Daniel couldn't understand that at all. The normal practice, if any disturbing noise came over the fence, was to turn on one's own hi-fi set as loud as possible, till the other party got the message.

But people didn't try that with the drummer. Those few who had tried it earlier quietly gave up.

But Daniel worried about Raja. He wasn't the sort to take this kind of thing for long. Raja was a man of many parts. You only had to see him, walking down the lane in a pair of shorts, a gold chain glistening on a cushion of hair on his barrel chest, to see that he always meant business.

He wouldn't stand any of this nonsense from anyone. Raja was not exactly the fellow Daniel thought of when he wanted to discuss a poem. But it was good to have someone like that as his neighbour; there weren't burglars in this neighbourhood, but it did give him a sense of security.

One day, as he returned home from work, Daniel knew

at once that something had gone wrong. So wrong as to shock the entire lane into an incoherent silence. He couldn't get much out of the first neighbour he met. But Raja was standing on the road, looking grim, his hands on his hips.

'Mr Silva's wife has disappeared,' Raja told him. Daniel looked at him, not understanding. What did he mean, disappeared? Mrs Silva was not the type of walk out on her husband just like that. They had been happily married for thirty-seven years.

'Nonsense, she didn't walk out on him,' Raja said, taking Daniel firmly by the shoulder. 'And that's not all. Look over there.' Daniel looked where Raja was pointing; there was a crowd down the lane, a little past Mr Silva's house.

'What's happening?' Daniel asked nervously. 'Come on,' Raja said firmly, and they walked down the lane. There were several armed policemen, questioning people, making notes. The crowd was looking at something pasted on a wall.

It was a life-size picture of Mrs Silva.

Mr Silva went about, sobbing, muttering to himself. Daniel tried to speak to him, but Mr Silva didn't seem to hear. And when Daniel talked to others, people who lived down the lane whom he had known for years, they shook their heads, or looked around, before muttering something unintelligible.

Daniel stared at the picture, fascinated. It was not a photograph; it looked more like a crude painting. But it was Mrs Silva all right. The words 'This is the fate of traitors,' were written across the picture.

As he walked back home, it suddenly occurred to Daniel that he hadn't seen the drummer. When Raja caught up with him, his barrel chest and hefty shoulders heaving with excitement, Daniel asked him whether he had seen the drummer.

'Bugger's there all right,' Raja said, 'sitting as quiet as

a mouse in his room.' But what did he mean? What did the drummer have to do with Mrs Silva's disappearance and the bizarre picture on the wall?

'None of the things are missing,' Raja said. 'I just spoke to the O.I.C.' He lowered his voice and said. 'Mrs Silva went to the cop station and lodged an entry against the drummer last week.'

Daniel stared at him in disbelief.

'Mr Silva was too scared to do it, so she went and told them this fellow was making too much noise.'

'So what did they do about that?' Daniel asked, not trying to hide his excitement.

'Not a thing,' Raja said. 'What do you expect the cops to do? He was the Silva's tenant. It's their problem.' Raja looked at Daniel for a long time, and finally said, 'It's high time somebody put an end to all this nonsense.'

But the drumming started that night; it seemed subdued, but it rolled on, ominously, like the heartbeat of a monster that had come to devour them all. Daniel had trouble sleeping that night. The drummer didn't sleep either. The drumming went on all night. Perhaps there were other drummers, and they took turns. Anything was possible.

There was no proof at all that the drummer had anything to do with Mrs Silva's disappearance. It was possible, though highly improbable, that she had walked out on her husband. Daniel even wondered if, like in those crime novels, Mr Silva had done in the old bag and had made up a story to pin the blame on someone else. But that was even more improbable.

In any case, the police had thoroughly searched the house, they had found nothing to connect either Mr Silva, or the drummer, with the disappearance of Mrs Silva. He wished they had. That would have made life seem less complicated for everyone concerned.

The drummer went on as if nothing had happened.

People began to avoid each other. In their dining rooms, they discussed 'certain horrible things' in the lowest of tones, and only with those they could trust their lives with.

And then, as it happened so often, the drumming mysteriously stopped. One morning, Daniel woke up with a start. It was six o'clock, and he was bleary-eyed. But there was no sound of drumming. Everything was so eerily silent. He began to pray that it would start, so that life could continue without becoming even more unbearable. But there was no drumming.

And the silence continued all day. On days like this, no one down the street was able to think clearly. They would have escaped to work, but it was a Sunday and they stayed in their houses like prisoners, edgy and awaiting the worst.

And then, towards the afternoon, there was a murmur outside. Daniel tried to ignore it; perhaps he was imagining it, and anyway strange noises weren't welcome. But the murmur grew steadily, and he couldn't stand it any more. He stepped out, to discover people running up and down the lane, excited.

There were armed policemen too, more than he had ever seen before. There was another crowd staring at the wall, where Mrs Silva's picture had been several weeks ago. It couldn't be the same picture, Daniel thought. The police had removed it the same day.

It was a picture of a young man, with the words 'trouble-maker' written on it. Daniel wondered who it was; the face was familiar. He tried to remember, and then someone murmured, 'the drummer.'

Of course. It was the fellow he had seen that day, the young man Raja had pointed out. But why was his picture on the wall now? Surely he couldn't have . . . . His neighbours shook their heads. The policemen were grim and silent. Mr Silva was there but there was no use asking him. He merely shook his head, looking more despondent than ever.

Raja! It suddenly occurred to Daniel that Raja wasn't there, among the crowd. That was very odd; Raja was the man who usually knew about these things. Daniel went back to his house and was startled to find Raja sitting in his living room. Before he could recover, Raja told him curtly, to sit down, as if Daniel was the guest. Daniel sat down. Looking around to make sure that no one was within hearing, Raja said, 'I did it.'

'You did what?' Daniel asked him, with a funny feeling in the pit of his stomach.

'I got rid of that drummer,' Raja told him heavily. 'Someone had to do it, no? None of you buggers have the guts, so I did it.'

The implications of this statement sank in fast enough. Daniel looked at Raja in disbelief. 'But how did you . . . ' he began, and Raja cut him short impatiently. 'Never mind how, you know why. Now we can all live in peace.' He stretched his arms luxuriously and yawned. They smiled at each other. It was a good time to open a bottle.

But the good feeling didn't last very long. Daniel didn't approve of violence. True enough, the drummer had been a nuisance, but was it necessary to 'get rid' of him? Daniel decided that it wasn't. And they had got used to the drumming. Now that it wasn't there, they were beginning to miss it. The silence was terrible.

And anyone who couldn't really stand the noise could have moved out. Daniel began to feel sorry for the drummer, and remembered that he was a harmless, insignificant little fellow who hardly dared to poke his head out of his room. Surely it wasn't necessary to do that?

Above all, he wished Raja hadn't told him about what he had done. Typical of the fellow, to go out and brag, instead of being modest about his achievements. The whole lane knew about Raja and the drummer's fate. It didn't really turn Raja into a hero. They began to avoid him as much as they had tried to avoid the drummer. The silence was getting on their nerves, and not all the stereos in the world could have helped soothe them.

Several weeks passed. Daniel tried to forget about the whole thing. But the sound of drumming that he routinely heard on the radio and on television shattered his composure and brought back memories of the drummer. He couldn't go on as if he knew nothing even if the others could. He had a conscience.

He had never liked going to a police station, but he was finally there, sitting on a comfortable chair in the O.I.C.'s room. The Inspector, a burly man with a thick moustache, was looking at him impassively. Daniel decided to get it over with as quickly as possible and leave the place. He was already regretting the fact that he had decided to come at all.

'It's somebody I know,' Daniel said. 'A man called Raja.'

'Friend of yours?' the Inspector raised his brows enquiring by.

'Sort of,' Daniel said. He began to cringe under the Inspector's gaze. 'But he told me—he admitted that he did it.'

'He did what?'

'I told you; got rid of the drummer.'

'What do you mean, got rid of? You mean he was killed?'

'That's for you to find out. I'm simply telling you what he told me.'

The Inspector was thoughtful for a moment. 'Well,' he said finally, 'suppose I told you that the drummer got rid of Mrs Silva?'

'I don't know about that,' Daniel said. 'Have you got any proof?'

'Let me ask you this,' the Inspector said with a smile.

'Do you have any proof that Raja got rid of the drummer?'

Daniel admitted that he hadn't. Raja had simply told him so.

'There you are,' the Inspector said triumphantly. 'So many people are saying that the drummer got rid of Mrs Silva.'

Daniel stared at the Inspector, who suddenly stopped smiling and leaned forward. He joined his thick fingers together, and said, 'Mr Daniel, you are a respectable citizen. I'm happy that you are here. You know that we have a very serious situation. Very serious. Now, do we understand that the drummer was disturbing the peace in your neighbourhood?'

'Yes, but . . . . '

'But what? Your friend has done something about it, so you can rest in peace now. Why don't you think of that?'

Daniel could find nothing to say.

'I'm not saying this is how it should have happened,' the Inspector added, frowning. 'We are here to take care of law and order. But, when someone has the common sense to help us a little, do you really have to complain?'

Daniel came out of the police station feeling dizzy. He had remembered too late that Raja knew the O.I.C. Now Raja would find out all about it. He wouldn't be able to face Raja again. My God, he thought, I'm going to leave this place and go away.

He saw the crowd in front of Raja's house. People stared at him as he approached. He saw Raja's wife, hysterical, being held with difficulty by some neighbours. People were looking at something on the wall, and no one went near it. He peered over somebody's shoulder.

It was a picture of Raja with the word 'traitor' written on it. And far away, somebody was drumming once again.

THE CHASM

The arrival of Vijay Ranawaka gave the little Sri Lankan community in Alice Springs a much-needed lift. He was from 'home'—they still thought of their former country as home. As a Sri Lankan, he roused in them a mixture of envy and self-satisfaction. Envy because he hadn't chosen to subject himself to the pain of self-uprooting; self-satisfaction because there he was sweating it out in the Third World, while they luxuriated in the sweet life of the First.

Vijay, a sociologist from Colombo University, was spending six months at the University of Sydney. Being a friend of Veeran Tampoe's brother automatically made him the prized possession of the Tampoes. Any Lankan guest offered opportunities for an entirely natural display of large quantities of crystal, silver, an elegant blue-and-white dinner service and a twelve-piece walnut dining-table unavoidable at the lavish meals the Tampoes felt so pleasantly obliged to ask every one to. Besides, it would have been sheer perversity not to make sensible use of Manel.

Manel was a nurse in the hospital Veeran Tampoe worked at as Registrar and had arrived from Sri Lanka eight months ago. A godsend to Nelun Tampoe, who had always hated cooking, washing, cleaning, in short, any sort of movement. Gracefully tall, with a mass of curly shoulder length hair, she had the elegance of a palace fresco meant to be strictly decorative. Unfortunately, not even electric mixers, choppers, juice extractors and microwave ovens had been adequate substitutes for a human cook. She had managed to survive the rigours of being an Australian housewife largely because her daughter, an atavistic quirk, loved cooking. But that daughter was now at Adelaide University, and only the timely arrival of Manel, a common or garden weed, had saved her from a situation which would have come dangerously close to crushing the lily on those occasions when hospitality demanded lavish meals. However, a price had to be paid: the token courtesy of an invitation. Manel wasn't exactly a servant. They hoped she'd refuse but she always accepted and joined in the conversation with the Mendises, the Ahameds and their other guests unselfconsciously, naturally, as if she really was one of them.

They enjoyed themselves on such occasions but there was always an ambivalence in their pleasure. They needed to be together, yet continually brooded over real or imaginary sins of omission and commission: the expected but unforthcoming invitation, the recipe purloined through devious questioning or the prospective guest purloined through pre-emptive hospitality. What really brought them together was Manel: she wasn't one of them. You could tell at once from how perilously close her 'ps' and 'fs' were whenever she spoke. How Manel *pried fotato-balls* was a joke which gave them a most pleasurable feeling of solidarity, the feeling that *they* were *they*. Looked at from this point of view her presence in their midst seemed almost an asset. They were often overcome by the starkness of their surroundings, so different from the land they'd left behind. A land of endless green expanses: paddy fields, palm-edged coasts, forests and jungles, tea-covered hill slopes, grassy plains; people everywhere, their houses, gardens and cattle. It was small, manageable and pretty. The vast bare plain surrounding the little enclave of Alice Springs overwhelmed them. The void outside transformed itself into a private panic they couldn't explain to themselves or to anybody else. Desperate, they sought affirmation of their being in familiar divisions and comfortable rivalries. But everything slipped beyond their control too easily, took unexpected turns, threatened to return them to an elemental nothingness, the unawareness of molecular chains innocent of *you* and *I*. And so the painful necessity of there being *you* to feel *I* they now felt as never before, though the smallness of their circle led to a kind of claustrophobia. Which is why the arrival of Vijay Ranawaka had been so invigorating. He was fresh blood.

Vijay, in Alice Springs for ten days, was now almost at the end of his holiday. There had to be a grand finale to round of all the numerous dinners and lunches given in his honour by everybody: dinners with Anglo-Australians and dinners without; rice-and-curry lunches and barbecue lunches. There had even been a breakfast—or was it a banquet?—with rice vermicelli and egg-hoppers, meat, fish, poultry and an array of pineapples, avocadoes and bananas. Razya Ahamed was exceedingly modest about the feast, she even apologized for the absence of mangoes. Unfortunately, they weren't available in Alice Springs at that time of the year.

The idea for the picnic came from Rudi Mendis. Yes, of course he knew there were no kangaroos or koalas in Standley Chasm the point of the place was the midday sun lighting it up. A colleague at the office had said it was quite spectacular. Hussein Ahamed suggested Ormiston Gorge. But Rudi had his way. So Standley Chasm it was.

On Thursday Veeran rang to say that the picnic party had an addition: Manel. Did they mind? 'No-o,' said Geetha. And then, 'But why?' The poor girl was bound to feel like a fish out of water—English wasn't her first language and picnics were so much more intimate than meals, weren't they? Veeran assured Geetha that Nelun and he would see to it that Manel didn't stray from her side of the social fence. But they really had to ask her, she'd been so very helpful these last ten days. After all, you had to be fair, hadn't you? Give the devil his due and all that. He gave a self-conscious little laugh. Geetha gave in.

The picnic party arrived at Standley Chasm shortly after nine o'clock. The two cars were parked and the food and drink distributed among the group. Manel carried Nelun's share as well as her own. 'What's in your tin, Manel?' inquired Rudi with interest. 'My favourite potato balls?' He gave Geetha a sly smile which she did not return.

'Well, what are we waiting for? Let's get going.' Veeran began walking past the kiosk towards the stony path leading to the chasm. The others followed. All around were gum trees—red gums, ghost gums and bloodwood with the occasional silver cassia and wattle. The wattles by the kiosk had burst into a million blooms, each tree a dense mass of lemon-yellow puff balls triumphing over all but a few brave blue-green leaves. Nelun broke off a spray, said, 'Isn't it beautiful?' and threw it away.

Manel looked alarmed. 'Don't do that. They might fine us for doing such things in these places,' she cautioned. Veeran was curt; 'I know how to handle such situations. Don't worry.'

'But—it is—it is the law in this country,' Manel said a little hesitantly.

'I don't need you for a teacher. Go and see if we've left anything in the boot of the cars. Go,' he said imperiously.

Manel looked distinctly taken aback. Neither Veeran nor any of the others had spoken to her like that before. She looked at them now, bewildered, then shrank into hurt silence, seeing no support in their cold or impassive faces. Rudi stepped forward, hesitated, stopped by the frown on Geetha's face. 'I'll—I'll go,' Vijay was saying, but Manel, who was already on her way to the cars, waved him back as he began to follow her.

Almost as taken aback as Manel, Vijay put Veeran's outburst down to Nelun's claim that Manel had insulted him the previous day. She'd said he was unethical. Geetha's reply, when Nelun had told her about it, was 'Didn't I tell you? Now we're stuck with her on our picnic.'

No one had ever exactly liked Manel. He'd noticed the suppressed smiles, the meaning looks; or simply the slight curtness brought on by something she'd said. Yet, they were civil, even gracious; she was grateful, always helpful. But deference? That they did not get. She didn't seem to understand that that was also expected of her. So beneath the civility there was the continual simmering. And then today this eruption.

Geetha had broken off a spray of wattle and had it defiantly stuck in the braided bun at the back of her head for the whole world to see. Slacks didn't suit her, thought Vijay. She was too plump. Manel, like Nelun, carried them off perfectly. He watched her walking to the car-park, held by the river of blue-black hair flowing down her back. She was very good-looking he decided, thinking of the covert glances, of lust rather than liking, Rudi Mendis often threw in her direction.

Hussein Ahamed sat down on one of the benches at the side of the kiosk, and turned on his transistor. 'Cricket commentary,' he announced. The others joined him.

'I'll have a look around,' said Vijay moving away. He wanted to get away from them. He had been touched by their hospitality at first; then overpowered by its excess. The covert intent of the Tampoe-Mendis-Ahamed probings concerning his family and friends had been nitially amusing, then irksome. Was he by any chance related to Jagath Ranawaka, the former Director of Health Services? Surely he must have known Jayaraj Rathnam and Maroof Cader if he'd been at Royal in the late fifties? Where had he read for his second degree? They conceded that Yale was almost as good as Oxford and Cambridge. He was one of them, they were satisfied on that point. Yet there was something about him that they were beginning to find disconcerting: the occasional expression suspiciously like amusement as they were talking about quite serious matters, his observations on men, manners and morals, these indicated not the outsider, but the apostate. Where his allegiances lay was what they now wanted to know. He didn't really know himself. In a society where ideologies and allegiances were being increasingly polarized, he had grown used to being in no man's land. He drew sustenance mainly from the ironical contemplation of himself and others, he reflected with wry ruefulness as he began walking back to the kiosk.

The others were still listening to the cricket commentary when he returned. The commercials came on, then a short news-break: an earth tremor registering 0.5 on the Richter scale was recorded early this morning in South-West Australia. The two Adelaide gaol escapees, Robert Pinn and Martin Morley, were reported to have been last seen in a blue Holden sedan in Alice Springs. The two men, who escaped a week ago, were serving ten year sentences on two separate counts of housebreaking and rape. Both men were armed and highly dangerous.

Manel came up panting slightly and said, no they hadn't left anything behind. The boots of both cars were empty.

'Well, then, let's get going,' said Rudi.

Ahead of them were trees, a boulder-choked path and the beginnings of rock walls which would merge with plateaus covered with clumps of grey-green spinifex further up. The Mendises and Ahameds walked on ahead of the others. Razya slowed down, stopped, and looked at the narrow path flanked by rock walls.

'What if—those—those escaped convicts—those rapists are hiding in the chasm.'

Hussein stared at her for a moment, drew himself up, flexed his muscles slightly. 'There are four men here, Razya. We should be able to deal with them.'

'But—but—they're armed.'

'Don't worry Razya, I can deal with rapists, armed or unarmed,' said Rudi ferociously. He'd been the University's champion boxer, and still looked a heavyweight.

'Come on, Razya,' said Hussein impatiently as he began walking briskly forward. Veeran and Vijay followed. Nelum and Manel, Manel helping Nelun over difficult patches, lagged a little behind.

Veeran talking about the social revolution back 'home' declared that, although he accepted progress, as a practical man of science he rejected the utopian dream of equality. Dictatorship and a lowering of the quality of life—that's what it led to.

'The illusory bait of equality and freedom, that is the opium of the masses,' announced Geetha, who finding the conversation interesting had dropped behind. She was a graduate, unlike the other women, and felt she could talk to the men as their equal. She often complained to Rudi that she found the other women either dull or unpleasant. Nelun was a pretentious doll, Razya good-natured but naive, and Manel argumentative.

After a moment's silence Vijay said, 'My idea of equality is social mobility. Everyone must have the chance to be a lawyer, even a Supreme Court Judge, the Prime Minister or . . . .'

'Yes, yes—that's why I like Australia,' said Veeran. 'My God, the money a doctor can make! The sky's the limit. The opportunities! But all this equality business has turned that girl's head. She forgets that there are boundaries which must be respected. I was saying to a medical colleague yesterday I'd open a path lab if I could, it's a goldmine, and she said, 'Entrepreneurial medicine is unethical', meaning that my intentions were unethical. What d'you think of that, uh?'

'It's obvious she has opinions of her own and isn't afraid to speak up. And in perfect English too,' said Vijay slyly.

'I know your type,' said Geetha, 'Right living, Left thinking.'

'That's one way of looking at it,' said Vijay stiffly beginning to fiddle with his camera, to look around. It was one way of escaping Geetha's comments. A place of contrasts, he thought. Contrasts in colour, shape and texture. The ochre-red of the mountains, the sky the usual blue, yet unusual in its luminous brilliance, blue falls pouring down floods of light; the terra-cotta of rock walls and boulders deepening to reddish brown. A place of myriad shapes. Boulders, spherical, rectangular, oblong; boulders like long rounded bolster pillows and the smooth roundness of small stones and pebbles. Mountains rearing into triangular peaks, declining into sloping shoulders and then the final flatness of level ground. Nature's primeval creations—megaliths, chasms and mountains—stark, abstract, were everywhere. A whirr of wings, a flash of blue and green. He focused his camera on the rosellas clinging to the palms plumaging the incline above: strange brilliant blooms.

Nelun caught up with her husband. Vijay dropped behind and joined Manel. They scrambled over great slabs of gleaming quartz and reddish boulders careful not to bruise hands and knees on the rough gritty surfaces. Now they were safely over a rocky hump and there before them was a bright channel of water, the water-lapped surfaces of the stepping stones offering precarious footholds to passersby. Rock faces rose on either side to become plateaus topped with boulders, clumps of spinifex and the occasional white-limbed ghost gum.

'What's that?' Razya looked up, terror in her voice, on her face.

'What? Where?' asked Hussein.

'I saw someone's head, something moved something—someone . . . . ' Her voice trailed away plaintively.

'There's no one, Razya,' said Hussein impatiently. 'It's all your imagination. Come on.'

Ahead, visible over the plateau, the mountains rose deep red against the sky. This is, thought Vijay, the beauty of the young earth preserved for a thousand million years. He almost expected a great earth beast to lumber down the mountain slopes or a dark bat shape, webbed wings outspread, sombrely surveying him, as it slowly circled ready to swoop. And he a grub, easily picked up and devoured. Then just before him was an enclosed space, a natural courtyard, its floor topaz and amethyst veined quartz. Three or four gums, their satiny greyish trunks disappearing in masses of dangling olive-green leaves, dappled the sunlight splashing down. A fallen tree lay on the ground. Razya and Nelun sat down thankfully.

'I'm dying for a beer,' said Rudi opening the esky. Razya leaned forward and peered in.

'Aah! Where's the pudding?' she demanded. Rudi looked at her inquiringly. 'It's not in here. I must have left it behind in the car,' she cried out.

'Didn't I ask you to check whether we'd left anything behind in the car?' Veeran turned to Manel.

'You didn't give me the car keys. I couldn't open the doors to look inside.' Manel spoke apologetically.

'Why don't we give her the keys and ask her to get the pudding from the car?' suggested Nelun, sipping her orange juice and fanning herself. 'Manel, get the pudding from the car,' she ordered.

Manel's expression changed, a slight but noticeable tightening of the lips. Refuse, refuse, intoned Vijay silently, Manel refuse. Manel said nothing; the others said nothing, simply looked at her. Go, said the collective will of the Tampoes, Mendises and Ahameds. Manel turned to go.

'No, no, no,' said Vijay, 'I'll go. Give me the keys.' He held out his hand.

'No,' said Manel quickly taking the keys from Geetha. 'I'll go.' Vijay drew back, startled by the fierce intensity countering the tremor in her voice, the glittering brightness of her eyes. She went. There was silence, an uncomfortable silence. Rudi lit a cigarette.

'Turn that damned transistor off. It's getting on my nerves,' snapped Geetha.

'I should've gone, I should have insisted on going,' said Vijay.

'Don't worry, it would've been useless. That women has a kind of toughness. Not exactly obstinacy but a—a kind of confidence,' observed Geetha grudgingly.

'She knew she had to go,' said Nelun calmly. 'She knew we brought her to help.'

Rudi continued smoking, drawing heavily on his cigarette, his eyes fixed on each spiralling ring of smoke. Why had Manel gone? Vijay asked himself. He had met her often in the last ten days, been drawn by her warmth, her openness. The warmth and openness springing from a life shaped by the seasonal regularity of almsgivings, weddings, New Year feastings, the casual dropping in on one another, all the easy gregariousness of village life. So here in Alice Springs, almost a village itself, maybe it was natural for her to look to the Tampoes, the Mendises and the Ahameds for that same convivial closeness. They had welcomed her, at least had seemed to. The mutual need was there. But the situation of friends suddenly turning imperious, that was disconcerting, difficult to deal with. You were sympathetic, helpful, because that was how you behaved to friends. So how do you meet imperiousness with peremptory refusal now? He saw her predicament, admired her restraint, but wished for rebellion.

He looked at the other picnickers fidgeting uneasily, wondered what new tensions would erupt, caught sight of a red-headed rosella and turned away with relief to watch it pecking away at invisible gum-nuts with its hooked predatory beak. A glittering haze wrapped the jagged red mountains rising before them, hurt their eyes. No one spoke. They listened intently to the silence vibrating like a bell.

It was Razya who spoke first, hesitant, timid. 'Do you think—I'm so so-o afraid to even think of it—what if—if those escaped rapists attack her?' She looked round nervously, her big dark eyes even bigger in her little face. The others knew whom she meant.

'Why should they attack her? Why should they be here at all?' demanded Veeran sharply.

'It's so easy to hide in this place—it's so lonely. And you can't—if—if you're attacked, there's no escape. You can't run with all these rocks on every side.'

'She'll be O.K. Geetha's right. She's a very obstinate woman. She insisted on going. We're not responsible for anything.' Veeran spoke loudly as if to drown the defensiveness in his voice.

Razya refused to be reassured. 'This place is frightening. All these rocks everywhere and these huge red mountains so close and the silence. I feel—I feel I'm in a kind of trap.' There was a sudden shower of sand and pebbles from above. Razya gave a little scream, Nelun jumped up, the men tensed. 'It's only a lizard,' said Geetha. They were silent again.

Vijay looking around for another scenic camera shot focussed on the cycad palms crowding the lower slopes of the red mountains and was back again, a boy at his grandfather's, holidaying on a coconut estate. The big event of that holiday had been the discovery of a dead woman in the jungle not far from the village, he remembered. He'd ignored the order not to join the stream of people flocking to the spot. Now he tried to forget that the woman's head had been severed from the sprawling naked torso, but the memory persisted. A river of black hair flowed on the ground, the wide-open eyes were glittering black mirrors. The other on lookers were disputing the cause of the killing: the deed of a betrayed lover said some; some said they knew who'd done it, and they'd done it to punish the woman for her arrogance; others wondered whether this was a sacrifice to the demon guardian of a treasure. That primitive savagery could still numb Vijay. He looked at his watch. Forty minutes since Manel had gone.

'What'll we do if—if anything happens to Manel,' whispered Razya, still anxious.

'If that what's-his-name—that Pin—Pinocchio dares touch a Sinhalese woman—any Sinhalese woman—I'll give him the bull-ant treatment so there'll be nothing left of his you-know-what. Mustn't offend the ladies by mentioning body parts,' said Rudi grinding his cigarette butt underfoot.

'Why only Sinhalese women? What about Tamil women?' demanded Veeran truculently.

'And Muslim women?' chipped in Hussein. 'I know half the world is anti-Arab, but we have our pride too.' Rudi ignored him.

'What I—I meant was—was any Lankan woman, so don't misunderstand, Veera. You're married to Nelun, so naturally I think of you as Sinhalese. You're like my brother.'

Veeran's glare showed plainly that this hasty declaration of brotherhood wasn't mollifying.

Hussein said he wasn't complaining but when morality was the keystone of the Islamic arch why was every one always criticizing the Arabs and calling them fanatical barbarians? Envy of the new flowering of Islamic culture, that's what it was.

'Aha, but you're not a practising Muslim, Hussein. You smoke, drink, eat pork, so where's your Islamic morality?' asked Geetha, maliciously triumphant.

Hussein ignored this thrust. 'Just let those rapists show their faces here—I'll smash their skulls open.' Picking up a large stone he hurled it against a boulder on the path opposite.

They're like primitives. No one at home will believe this, thought Vijay. Maybe they're feeling guilty about Manel, sending her off like that. Or was the cause deeper? There was here the rage, the frustration of the dispossessed. The supermarket cornucopia, the electronic plenty were there; they laughed all the way to the bank. Yet deep within, they were dispirited. The landscape, its endless flatness broken only by huge humps of rock or deep clefts, overwhelmed them. They talked to people. An exchange of sounds with no engagement of the spirit.

'There's Manel. At last!' cried Vijay. He hurried to take the pudding from her.

'We were so-o worried about you,' claimed Razya ingenuously.

'Why?' There was an unusual sharpness in Manel's

voice. Then with unexpected acuity she asked, 'Did you thing I was murdered?'

No one answered.

'If we don't hurry, we'll never see the sun over Standley Chasm,' said Rudi. He began to walk. The others followed.

They reached the towering walls just as they were being transmuted into massive spurts of red-black solidifying lava, the daily recreation of that cataclysmic eruption of a thousand million years ago. Thirty seconds past twelve. The volcanic fires faded as they watched. The splendid moment of primordial mimicry had come and gone. The party began to walk down the path to the rocky alcove where the food had been left. Vijay and Manel lingered behind for a minute or two.

'Why did you go and get the pudding, Manel? Why didn't you refuse?'

'I didn't know how to. It—it seemed rude and ungrateful when I've eaten so often in their houses to just say, I can't. I thought they liked me. Because if they didn't, why invite me so often? Today, I felt they were punishing me for something. But for what, I don't know.'

'Come and eat,' called out Geetha. 'Vijay, the foods ready.'

Vijay looked at Manel, 'You go,' she said, 'It's you they're calling.

'No,' he said firmly, 'you must come too. Come.'

She followed reluctantly.

Geetha was removing the thick layers of newspaper she'd used to keep the foil-wrapped packets of savoury rice and curried chicken warm. She handed a packet to Vijay.

'Ladies first,' he said, handing the packet to Manel.

'Manel, give that packet to Razya,' said Nelun.

'Let her have it,' said Razya. 'She brought the pudding for us.'

Manel looked at the packet she held in her hand. Slowly, she put it back on the plastic square spread out on the rock. Vijay looked at her inquiringly. She shook her head apologetically, then looked at the others.

'You asked me to your picnic. That was kind of you because I know we are very different people. You are rich and educated. So maybe you thought me a fool. And maybe I was a fool to think you liked me. But I am a simple village woman. To me your ways are strange. So I think I'll leave your picnic now.'

The picnic party gaped. Vijay made a movement, got up.

'No,' she said, looking at him. 'I can find my own way back.' She ran lightly down the rough-hewn steps of the slope, passed between the chasm's towering walls, disappeared.

Hussein was the first to break the silence. 'How about some music?' he asked resolutely bright. Without waiting for replies, he slipped a cassette into the transistor.

'Bit high-and-mighty leaving us like that, don't you think?' Veeran looked at the others for confirmation.

'No, she's not proud, she's humble. She said she was a villager,' insisted Razya, seizing on this crumb of comfort.

'You haven't got the point, you're taking her literally. She was being sarcastic, I didn't think she could,' said Geetha.

'And in English too,' Vijay said, smiling sweetly.

'What's happened is that Roger Moore's attentions have gone to Manel's head. Thinks she's already a surgeon's wife and riding her high horse. These Aussies—decent chaps and all that—but a bit dense when it comes to the finer points of birth and breeding.'

'My God, what a bonanza for that woman!' exclaimed Nelun. 'You never even hinted at such a thing, Veera, and now you drop this bombshell on us just like that.' Her breathing quickened audibly. 'My father was a

Professor of Law and my grandfather was a Supreme Court Judge,' she announced.

'What's that got to do with anything?' demanded Geetha rudely.

Nelun's lower lip quivered uncontrollably.

'It has everything to do with what's just happened, Geetha,' said Veeran. 'Manel can change her civil status, but she can never change her ancestry.'

'Do such things matter if you've got self-respect and dignity?' asked Vijay challengingly, 'Chuck ancestry into a museum of antiquities. That's where it belongs along with the battle-axe and chain-mail armour.' He felt a thrill of ferocious pleasure as he spoke.

'Time to get going, don't you think?' asked Hussein getting up. 'I've had enough of this chasm. Let's go now, let's go.'

There was little talk among the picnickers on the way back. An occasional, 'It's so-o hot,' or 'Don't walk so fast, Veera, I can't gallop like a horse,' from Nelun was all that could be heard.

Vijay was busy with his own thoughts. He was struck by the bluntness of the talk of a little while ago. Conversations at home were conducted with subtlety and finesse. For the Right People, the discreet compliment, the tactfully offered service, the deferential attention; for the Ordinary, civil patronage. But, what was delicately muted there was brassily loud here. Was this the price they paid for the sweet life? This self-parody? Half-saddened, half-amused, he added Nelun's proclamation and what had followed to his collection of traveller's tales.

They arrived at the kiosk around three and went in for tea, cakes and picture postcards. Vijay went up to the cash-register. Had by any chance a young Asian woman called in earlier on in the afternoon? Yes, there'd been one. She'd left with Jack, who was going into Alice for the weekly groceries.

'Here's Jack back already! Heh, Jack, drop that lass safely back in Alice?'

'I sure did. Had a nice natter on the way.'

'I knew she'd be all right,' Veeran was saying, 'she can look after herself,' while Vijay thinking of the possible transformation of Manel into Mrs Roger Moore felt a qualm. Would she in time become like these others? How could one really say?

The picnic party finished their tea and cakes, bought their postcards and were ready to leave. The Mendises and Ahameds shook hands with Vijay. 'Have a good trip to Sydney,' they said. He noticed the absence of the conventional hospitality formula—the polite request to come again. But he knew that the chill, the discreet distances now evident would pass; after a while the round of dinners, lunches and picnics would begin again. And so it would go on.

A Pair of Birds

Raja found it finally, buried it the debris, lodged between the fallen rubble. He picked it up carefully, wiping it gently with his palm. Without its blue backdrop wall, against which it had been hanging for as long as he could remember, it had lost its colour. The flying white birds had lost their vibrance, they looked washed out, their fluid motion as they flew into the sky, did not seem quite lifelike now. The picture was dirtied anyway. He was so tired, washed out, like the pair of birds in the picture. He would sit down a moment. The air was full of human ashes and screams and cries. It was lonely and silent.

Two children came up along the road, with dirty faces and ragged frocks. Seeing him, they passed on, turned in at the next burnt-down heap of a house, and began, with hurried alert eyes, to look round. They had their dreams. Perhaps they would find beneath a brick or stone, a thali, or a bangle. How wonderful that would be.

'There's nothing at all here,' said the elder child, 'Someone has already beaten us to it.'

They stood together forlornly, it was the last probable treasure store down the lane, except for the charred ruins on which this tiresome man sat. They stared at him. Would he move? Perhaps he would not mind, if they searched there too.

'Look around this place. You might find something. See, I found this,' he said to them, 'You might be luckier.'

They came up to him warily. He did not seem to be from the police. They took the picture from him and looked at it.

'Oh what use is this old burned picture?' they scoffed, gaining confidence.

'You can't sell it for anything. Not like finding a brass vase or a gold ring. Like Sunil's finding. He's rich now, he sold the thali to the *mudalali,* and he has enough money to get married with.'

'Who is Sunil?'

'Our brother. He's been collecting money to get married, for as long as I can remember. He's the scavenging man, who pushes the garbage cart down this road. It does not pay, you see,' the child finished maturely.

He wished the children would go away now and leave him alone. Making hay while the sun shines, he thought. The buried hatred and fury surged within him again. The children moved away, and with a stick began to dig among the charred remains of his house. He picked up a heavy stone; if he threw it at them now, at least one would be hurt. What part of which body could he aim at? The head, or the leg? Out of another body, another cry would pierce the evening quiet. He stood up, lifting the stone over his shoulder, poised to throw it. There was a singing in his ears, he heard the shouts, the screams, his mother and his sister, dragged out of the house by their father, the men with their crowbars and sticks, maddened faces and shining sweat-covered bodies in the darkness. And then the splintering glass, the blood gushing out of his father's head, where they had struck him, the burning. The fire eating in, spreading into the bedrooms, to his books, enveloping all. The two children had turned, they were gazing at him innocently.

'There's nothing here, Sir,' they said, 'We are going home.'

He dropped the stone. And sat down again. Drained out, empty.

He shook himself, he had come here to think. Not to relive the past. What was there of the past anyway? His father was dead, his mother and sister in the refugee camp. He had to plan, as the head of his family now, he had to plan, settle things for his mother and sister. Where could he start? Menik wanted them to come and stay with her family. But in her kind offer he saw only patronizing. He visualized his mother and sister, sitting hidden away in a back room somewhere, eating out of the left-overs in the house. He was only working himself up again. He tried to calm down, and dropped his head in his hands. He was being unnecessarily cruel now, he admonished himself, he knew Menik, she only wanted to help. So many of their other Sinhalese friends wanted to help. Lal, Maithri, they had been with him round the clock, after they had heard of the tragedy. He had been abrupt, cold and unfriendly. Perhaps he had hurt them, cut them off altogether. He could not help it. He wondered if he had been foolish. Perhaps he should have accepted their help. He was really helpless. They had just this ten thousand rupees in the bank, and his sister's dowry, awaiting her marriage. He could not touch that, it was a sacred fund. And he had his job. They could seek political asylum in England or France, he thought.

He stood up and wandered on, down the road to Maithri's house. He felt embarrassed, were they on two sides now? But Maithri had offered his house to his family during the riots and they had been friends for nearly ten years, classmates, neighbours, and had Maithri's father not been working in Jaffna, he was sure, the destruction of his house would never have taken place. He remembered suddenly, with a flash of gratitude, how Mr Seneviratne had taken special care of them in the last riots of '81. Well, it was worth a try anyway, it might ease the misery in his heart, if he could communicate it to Maithri. Share it with him.

Maithri stood by the gate of his home. He looked around moodily—three houses down his lane, all of them saved in the last riots, because of his father, lay in ashes today. Our peaceful nation, he thought, our religious people, how violent they were when it came to a national problem. He remembered having read somewhere about how the Sinhalese reacted violently to injustice—quick to anger, quick to forget. For the past how many years, had this ethnic problem been brewing beneath the surface? Yet, they had grown up, side by side, the Sinhalese and the Tamils, he and Raja. What had nationality to do with friendship? They had hidden three Tamils in their house during the last week, friends from the front house, Shanthi too. He wondered if their friendship could be love. He liked everything about her, the way she walked, the way she talked, the way her vivacious eyes met his, half shyly, half coquettishly when he spoke to her. But last week they had fled to Jaffna. Nothing remained for them here, the house lay in desolation, broken, half burnt walls and flapping windows, like the skeleton of some grotesque animal, exposed to sun and rain. He heard the postman's bell. He learned over the gate. But the postman did not stop at his house.

'Nothing today, Sir,' he smiled sympathetically and rode on.

Maithri felt, more than saw, his mother's shadow move away from the window. From morning she had been hovering about the verandah waiting for the letter that failed to come. From his father in Jaffna. Was anything wrong, he wondered for the hundredth time, why was there not even a phone call? But perhaps the telephones were out of order in Jaffna. He had tried to call last evening but failed. Perhaps they should try sending across a police message tonight. But no news meant good news, he thought again. And his father must be very busy. He looked up and down the lane, restlessly.

Jaffna. What was Jaffna like today? His thoughts dwelt again inexorably on his father. Usually, he skirted this issue, and filled his mind with lesser things. But now. How was his father? His mother's worried face made him want to avoid her, they were helpless here, they could do nothing but wait, wait for news that he was still alive, wait for news that he was shot dead. He remembered reluctantly, painfully, the argument that had taken place between his mother and father, the day his father brought home his transfer orders. He was to take command in Jaffna the next day. His mother had been so angry.

'You have no right to go away to Jaffna. You have two children. They will have a dead father in a week, if you go. It is just a death trap, Jaffna, you said so yourself yesterday. See what happened to Wije and Gunadasa . . . where are they now with their heroics? Dead. Ashes. And where are their families? Forgotten. You can't afford to die for your country when you have a family. Of what use is a dead hero?'

'Look, Chitra, I am not trying to be a hero. It is important that you understand that. It is just that I am a police officer and I have a job to do. How can I get the transfer cancelled at this moment? I have no choice in the matter at all. I am in the police, you know.'

'They will kill you, Lal, you know what the terrorists are. Tell Suren, he will get the transfer cancelled. There must be so many others who have not served in Jaffna yet. Who are free and unmarried, let them go.'

But there had been no hesitation in his father's voice, no indecision when he said. 'It is out of the question, Chitra, you know it, let's not get hysterical about it, I'm not on some suicidal squad, and really not cut out to be a hero. And you can't forget my horoscope—I'm to live to be a good eighty years, remember? Nothing is going to happen to me.'

His father had not been joking. His voice was strained with the tensions of his work. Had he been trying to convince his mother or himself?

And when he had been taken away in the jeep, with his single suitcase of clothes, his last thoughts had been of them at home.

'Be very careful, don't go out at night, Maithri, look after your mother and sister. I leave you in charge. Just be careful, I will write to you as soon as I can.'

As the jeep turned the corner, he had looked back, and Maithri had been surprised, his father was not a sentimental person. He was afraid for his father. And filled with anger for these terrorists who created all this havoc in the country. Eelam my foot, Maithri thought furiously, separatism, division, all words—we have to fight them, they must not break up our country. 'Let Shanthi go to hell,' he said aloud, angrily.

*

He did not see Raja until Raja stood in front of him. The two gates were closed. Raja stood just outside on the road. Maithri looked at his friend. He opened the gate.

'Hello, come in Raja, I was thinking of something and didn't see you really.'

He smiled, his arm went around Raja in a familiar gesture. But Raja felt Maithri's effort. They had been friends for too long for either to pretend anything. Yet, just now pretence was necessary, and so he smiled a smile he did not really feel.

'Sit down. *Nangi,* bring something for Raja to drink, he's looking hot and sweaty.'

His sister came in a few minutes later with a glass of fruit juice. She served it to him, smiling—she liked Raja, they were like brothers—Raja and *aiya* She sat down on the arm of a chair.

'It must worry you that schools are still closed, *nangi.* There isn't much time left for your exam now, is there?' Raja tried to make conversation. Examinations, he thought, it was a topic that was safe. Impersonal.

'Just two months more. We have not even covered all the syllabuses yet but it's not so important. We are all so worried about *thaththa* being in Jaffna . . .' she said wistfully. 'We have had no news from him for three days. Perhaps he has no way of sending a message across. Nothing in the post today too, *aiya.*'

'I know,' Maithri said.

They sat together quietly. They had never been quiet like this in the past, Raja thought, they would all talk together, and Maithri's mother would sometimes shout from the house—'Make less noise, people will think there is a street brawl in the house.'

But they would not care. Now this silence, was stretching, stretching before them, yawning into nothing.

'So, how are Auntie Rose and Saku? You should have brought them here, Raja, they would have been safe with us, they could at least have eaten some good food.'

'Thank you. They are doing very well at the camp. At least, they are not feeding on scraps falling off someone's table.

Raja's mouth was dry by the time he uttered the last word. He cringed, seeing the hurt gather in Maithri's sister's eyes.

'Maybe it's for the best, *Nangi,* I don't suppose *thaththa* is being treated kindly by those Tamils in Jaffna;' Maithri returned, furiously.

They sat tongue-tied, staring at nothing. Confused. Uncertain of what next to say. Damn these Tigers.

'But Shanthi's family is in Jaffna too, isn't it? They will take care of him.' Raja resumed the conversation, with an effort.

'If the terrorists let them. If those devils find out that Shanthi's family is helping a Sinhalese, they'll all be shot,' Maithri said.

'Was nothing left of your things? No books, nothing?' Maithri wished that his sister would shut up. But Raja did not seem to mind. He showed her the picture of the birds.

'This is all I could find. Maybe the looters were luckier.' He could not keep the bitterness from his voice.

'You are lucky your lives were saved,' Maithri cut in again, he could not help it, there was this anger in him, they had no business to sound like holy martyrs, he thought, it was their own people who started all this and someone had to pay the price. Why should it be his father? Better the Tamils themselves, and Raja was a Tamil. Maybe in his secret heart he was himself a Tiger, or wishing that he was one.

'You would not say that, had you seen everything going up in flames that night. Or were you with the mob yourself? I did not know that your sympathies were with them,' exclaimed Raja.

He gripped the arms of his chair. What was the meaning of this? They were arguing, weren't they? So they were now irrevocably on either side of the dividing line. The Tamils and the Sinhalese. Doesn't he care that my mother and sister are starving, homeless in the camp?

How can Raja forget, Maithri wondered, very hurt, how he had begged him to bring his family to this house.

They were both angry and full of resentment.

'Come, now, what is the matter with the two of you? You can't settle the country's problems, don't be idiotic.

You'll be hitting each other in a minute,' Maithri's sister said, she went away into the house. She was getting a little tired of it all. But she could not blame anyone. Could she?

Maithri's mother came towards them a few minutes later. She carried a basket covered with paper.

'I have prepared some food for Rose and Sakuntala, Raja, you can take it along with you to the camp when you go.'

She sat down sighing, trying to think of something to say. She felt the tension in the air. But her thoughts returned to what was uppermost in her mind.

'I don't know when these problems will settle down, I was listening to the news just now, there is a forty-two hour curfew imposed in Jaffna starting at noon today. *Thaththa* must be in such danger.' Her voice trailed away. She sat staring into nothing, into the distance. There was nothing, really, that one could do, but wait and hope and pray. Raja stood up.

'Thank you for the food, auntie,' he said taking the basket, 'it is kind of you to have bothered.'

'Tell Rose and Saku that I will come to see them soon,' she tried to smile. 'It's just that I am so worried about Lal.'

'Of course, I'm sure they will understand. Don't worry about it.'

Raja moved towards the door. He glanced at Maithri. Maithri stood up with an effort.

'I'll just go up the lane with Raja', he said to his mother.

'Come right back,' she admonished quietly.

They walked together up the lane.

'Smoke?' Maithri offered his half-smoked cigarette to Raja.

'Sorry, *maching*, it's this *thaththa's* being away that keeps getting us down,' He tried clumsily to make up.

Raja was silent. They were passing his house.

'I think of your father too, had he been here, my house would have been safe. We keep thinking about that, back in the camp. He is a good man, your father. When did we ever argue about nationality before this. It is just this . . . let's forget it. What can you and I do anyway, from here.'

Maithri saw Raja to the bus.

'Don't come this way tomorrow. It is not safe to wander around by yourself. I will bring something for you to the camp.' Raja did not reply immediately.

'Thanks,' he said, at last, trying to sound grateful. Maithri watched the bus out of sight. Then sticking his hands in his pocket he moved away.

As he neared his house, he saw the police car parked by the gate and the small group of people gathered by it. He stopped walking and stood rooted to the gravel. He bit his lip desperately. He saw his sister extricate herself from the clutching hands of friends. She came running towards him. She stopped before him. He drew her to him and held her tightly. He looked beyond the gate. He saw his mother walk into the house surrounded by neighbours.

'A land mine,' his sister sobbed.

THE WISDOM TREE

Nobody knew why Tikka suddenly decided to change his ways, not even his closest cronies Sadath and Jumu. It was a mystery to them and he never told them although they plied him with questions. Why should a chap full of fun and laughter, playing truant from school and enjoying life all day long suddenly become a model of good behaviour?

Tikka was everybody's bugbear; his mother thought he was incorrigible, but Tikka's *achchi* Alice Nona was not of the same mind. His birth chart promised greatness and good fortune and she simply doted on him. Once when they asked him why he had changed, he replied 'I learned wisdom from a tree' but he wouldn't say which tree and they couldn't think of any tree that could be called a Wisdom Tree either.

Although Tikka was the apple of his grandmother's eye no one could have said that his feelings for her were reciprocal. He took her as young boys of his age are wont to do, very much for granted or maybe his feelings could be described as cupboard love, for he loved the unfailing gifts she brought him. Tikka would stay out of the house without returning even for a meal but he was back every evening demanding his gift.

Alice Nona had quite a reputation in the *vaththa* where they lived. It was a slum area but a respectable slum area, right in the heart of Colombo, full of Middle East returnees and the ubiquitous radio set was found in every dwelling. In most big cities in the world, manifestations of poverty are to be found cheek by jowl with manifestations of affluence, but while opulence sprawls out with assurance and dignity; poverty is discovered sulking and lurking in alleyways.

A stone's thrown from the little alley leading to the slum was the *Maha Iskolaya* 'the biggest and best boys' school in Sri Lanka' as Alice Nona was fond of calling it. The school the other 150 or so slum children attended was further away from the big sprawling establishment which had been founded by suddhas. According to the government regulations if you lived within a certain radius of the school precincts, your sons were entitled to a place in the school. It was Alice who unearthed this priceless piece of information and it gave her no rest. It was said that she had paid all her savings to a policeman married to a friend of her daughter's, and with his help secured birth certificates, identification forms, marriage certificates, electricity bills and a couple of recommendations from the right 'connections' to prove that they had indeed lived there all their lives. She went for an interview with her daughter and son-in-law, spoke boldly in Sinhala when they addressed her in English and was not at all inhibited by their questions or daunted by the 'perfumed mothers and tiepinned fathers' who turned up for interviews in limousines driven by liveried chauffeurs. Finally Tikiri Bandara's name was added to the register of students in year one.

The Wisdom Tree

Alice Nona's exertions did not cease. She bought him a pair of blue shorts, a shirt, a pair of shoes, socks, a lunch box, a drink bottle, an exercise book and as a special gift a pencil box which she had observed was a *sine qua non* among school children.

Tikka however, though he left for school with a swagger, did not appear to like school as much as expected. Day after day he returned home crestfallen.

One day he returned even before school closed for the day—he was bruised, his drink bottle missing, his book torn and his pencil box broken. Locked in Tikka's heart was the memory of why he never wanted to go to school again. The class teacher had demanded certain information from the boys including occupations of parents and addresses. The boys sat up and looked with renewed respect at those who didn't have to resort to mumbling, but mentioned with pride who their fathers were. One boy turned out to be an M.P.'s son. Tikka confessed that his father had no job and that he lived in the *vaththa* behind the school. Later, places were changed: Tikka who had bagged a place in the front row was relegated to the last row. The M.P.'s son was appointed class monitor and given his place. Later the boys discovered that Tikka's wooden pencil box was empty. Amused, they passed it from hand to hand and then used it as a football. The headmaster walked in and pulled up the class monitor. Tikka discovered that life in school could be hell.

Tikka's parents gave up trying to make him attend school. They knew that Tikka was capable of living by his wits like his father. It was amazing what he could do, the stunts he would pull to rake in the extra buck. He haunted the market place. Rich foreigners, diplomats' wives were accustomed to seeing a dark little boy spring forward with a wide grin and relieve them of their baskets. He'd carry their goods back to the car, bid them good day flashing a winning smile and be rewarded with a fat tip. The men at the fruit stalls and vegetable stalls kept him supplied with bribes to make him bring customers to them. They preferred to give their over-ripe fruit to Tikka for services rendered, rather than sell it them for less. Often his family enjoyed a palatable soup made from bones from the meat stalls and a couple of tomatoes from a vegetable seller.

He had other tricks up his sleeve as well. He could twist his ankle and bend the fingers of one hand to make it look stiff, then he would place a crutch in his arm pit and drag one leg. His friends would hoot and laugh at his tricks. Once he had got a hundred rupee note from a foreigner after rendering in faltering English a long list of misadventures. Tikka never baulked at drowning his father at sea, losing his mother in giving birth to him or losing any member of his family in a fire if it could get him a rupee.

He had also designed a special costume to be used when he needed a change of scene. In a torn shirt and a trouser, both strangers to soap and water and held together by numerous safety pins, with a rusty old tin he would board a train to Kandy or Galle and beg from the passengers. In a train the response was good. The passengers couldn't shake him off, they were embarrassed to abuse him in front of strangers, they liked to pretend they were generous souls and some even tried to outdo the others; some were bored or they just wanted to get rid of him. Tikka rejoiced in his irregular ways.

Alice Nona did everything possible to bribe her Tikiri back to the *Maha Iskole*. Once he dressed up and set out with his grandmother who waited and watched him walk in through the gates to make sure he wouldn't play truant. She worked in the Big House close to the Maha Iskole and when she returned at six-thirty in the evening she called him her *rattaran putha* and gave him

The Wisdom Tree

the coins for an ice cream as promised, Later she heard from his friends that he'd been at the beach and had flown kites the whole day.

It was a long established habit of the grandmother to bring a 'little something' for her precious Tikiri from her place of work everyday. The people she worked for were very kind and generous. They had big dogs and the *mahathaya* was a *lokka* who went to Parliament, but it was surprising how good they were to her. They were somewhat strange and unpredictable in the kind of presents they gave. Sometimes they were expensive; a toy, a saucer, a spoon. Sometimes it was a cracked bottle or mug. One day it was a single marble. All his treasures had come from the Big House—broken ornaments, a ball, erasers, a cracked mug, a couple of dice. She said that Tikiri should not tell anyone how generous they were at the Big House because the people in the *vaththa* would taken *vaha* and she would lose her job, so he never did. The best gift had been a real camera—quite a small one, but no one had known how to use it. Tikka had managed to make it click a few times and a flash of light had lit up the place when he pressed a button the first time, surprising everyone. He couldn't get it to light again so his father said it was best to sell it. Tikiri wanted to keep it and asked his *achchi* to find out from the lady who gave it how to use it—but she got a good price for it instead. Hundred and fifty rupees was not to be sneezed at.

Tikka's favourite pastime was to listen to his grandmother relate stories about the two children in the Big House. Both were boys. One his age and the other older. The treated her well and gave her gifts. They called her *achchi* and pretended she was their grandmother. They never ate chocolate, cake or ice cream without giving her a share, but they liked to see her enjoy it, so Tikka never got a taste of it. Often she would describe the Big House. The toilets alone were each the size of their own house. The enormous bedrooms had picture paper on the walls. The two fridges and deep freezes were crammed with food. She was most struck by a large room which only contained shelves and shelves of books, nothing more except for a few vases, each said to be worth thousands and thousands of rupees. She described the owner of the place, an old man who would pore over the books all day, using a magnifying glass since his eyes were weak. Some of the books weighed at least ten pounds each—you had to draw your chair up to a table and rest the book on the table. It was too heavy to be held while it was read.

Alice Nona had a great deal of reverence for the written word. 'If you learn to read you will one day own a house as big as that' Alice Nona would wind up her story every day.

One day Tikka's mother called out to him 'Tikiri be a good boy; your grandmother has left her betel pouch and gone to the Big House. If you run quickly you can catch up with her before she walks in through the gates.' Tikka raced off but fell in with some friends and forgot his errand. At the end of the day (they had eaten *kadalay* and pineapple pieces with *miris kudu* for lunch on Galle Face Green) he felt the pouch in his pocket and realized how remiss he had been. Quickly he sped towards the Big House. If he met his grandmother on the way home he could escape a scolding from his mother. He stood at the entrance dwarfed by the enormous wrought iron gates. His *achchi* was still inside. The security shed was empty and enormous spikes jutted out of the twelve foot wall as far as he could see on all sides. He rattled the gate and dogs began to bark. Two alsatians and a bulldog appeared with a gardener who shouted 'Get out of here before I break your bones.' Tikka decided to walk along the wall to the other side.

The Wisdom Tree

He guessed he was in the kitchen area when he heard the sound of someone pounding flour. He noticed a large tree nearby and in a flash he had clambered up and perched himself on a branch. No one had seen him. He peered through the branches.

The first thing he noticed was that it was his grandmother who was pounding flour. This surprised him as she had been falling ill lately and in the last few years had often developed a pain in the chest. She had been warned never to carry weights. Tikka thought he would frighten her by throwing something near her. His hand closed round a small twig. He was taking careful aim when a lady dressed in a bright sari came out of the house. His *achchi* pounded on with renewed vigour.

He almost fell out of the tree when the lady began to shout at his grandmother in a shrill voice. He could not hear everything but it was clear that she was accusing her of being lazy and shirking her duties. After sometime she turned on her heel and stalked off. Presently his *achchi* scraped up the last of the flour into a newspaper. She rested for a moment brooding, then took her parcel and walked slowly towards the door. She stopped when she heard a terrible clamour. Three dogs and two young boys both carrying bows and arrows came sweeping down upon her. In the younger of the two he recognized his class monitor. With fierce howls they fell on her frightening her out of her wits. The parcel flew from her hand and the flour was sprinkled in the dust. Making fearful noises they danced round the old woman who threw her arms about to ward off their blows. The dogs barked and made a fearful din. Finally the bigger boy pulled out his gun and fired at her from point blank range. When he was satisfied that the 'carcass' of his quarry was riddled with bullets, he withdrew his dogs and they disappeared round the corner of the house laughing loudly and derisively.

He watched his grandmother try to salvage what she could from the dirt. The lady came out and screeched at her over again. Tikka noticed for the first time how old and frail she looked. He had never noticed before how small and bent and shrivelled up she was. She was told that she would have to pound rice all over again the next day. She had not said a single word. She bent and wiped her eyes with the corner of her cloth. Tikka found that his cheeks were wet too. He watched her sweep the yard once more and at last she had picked up her reed bag and wrapped her fresh cloth round her waist. All the while she dabbed at her eyes with the corner of it. The lady came out once more, paid her daily wage and then examined her bag. It smote him sorely to think that his *achchi*, was being treated like a common thief. The lady watched her till she had disappeared round the corner of the house.

Tikka was about to drop down when he noticed that his grandmother had stopped. Something in her movement arrested him. She was looking over her shoulder surreptitiously. Then she walked up to the dustbin and he saw her bend and rummage in the garbage. At last she found what she had been looking for. She looked around once more and then tucking the object into her blouse she walked quickly to the gate.

Tikka sat there a long while. When he clambered down at last the lamps along the roads were lit and vehicles had their headlights on. It was very late. He ran home and reached his doorstep just after his *achchi*. His mother was already rebuking him for not delivering the pouch. For once he did not demand his gift from his grandmother. He saw that her face was wreathed in smiles. 'See what the little boy in the Big House gave me just because I told him I liked it. It is for you' and reaching into her blouse she took out a bright little car. It was very attractive but Tikiri's joy, her doting yet discerning eye noted, was not as spontaneous as she had expected.

And she was the first to notice the great change in her grandson that everybody was to remark about afterwards. She looked at him for a long time and read a message in his eyes that told her that he was too big for gifts from the Big House now. That was the last gift she brought him and she said it was because he never needed to be bribed again.

WEDDING IN THE FAMILY

I first heard of the wedding the night I woke to my mother's soft weeping. Father was angry and his voice was quick and soft. The angrier he was, the softer and quicker he spoke. Sometimes other people did not know he was angry. But then, he got angry so seldom.

That night he was really angry. I rolled over to the other side of the mat on the floor and tried to cover my ears. But the words came seeping in. They did not make much sense. But my mother's weeping did. I did not care for the words my father said, but I cared about those heartbreaking sounds that came from my mother. They did not even know I was awake, that I had heard . . . .

Next day several people came to the house and they talked of the wedding as if it as a funeral. My grand-aunt, the school teacher, said that the wedding was a bad omen. The first wedding in the family, the eldest son getting married this way and so many younger ones . . . the girls may never be able to get married after this disgrace, she said. If only everyone had taken some

Wedding in the Family

trouble and got at least the eldest girl married early it wouldn't have mattered so much, she said darkly. Now, that will become of all these young ones, she asked. It is their karma, she said, resigned and sighing, her thin chest heaving with this heavy burden.

The spectre of so many girls becoming old maids in some distant future set many of the visitors talking, all at once. They dug up several families where the women were still unmarried, wasting their lives at home, fighting over property and ill-treating their brothers' wives, step mothering their children, getting old and dried up. Poor old Adeline aunty's six daughters were all at home, a real burden on the old widow.

What had happened was, one whispered to another, their brother, the oldest in *that* family too, had married a Burgher girl from Galle and that was what happened . . . she was fair and had blue eyes and wore frocks and spoke in English, of course. But none of the marriage brokers ever came to the house on the hill after *that* marriage!

Father's younger sister who lived on the adjoining land was close to tears. She remembered how she had carried this favourite eldest nephew when she was a teenager and he was so little. How she had bathed him and fed him, loved him and petted him. How on some days he would cry that the stones hurt his little feet when he wanted to be carried on her shoulder, his arms hugging her tight round her neck. And now here he was, a grown man, getting married and to a girl she had never seen, a girl who was not suitable at all, at all, she wept.

It was she who came across the fields to our house early on the morning of the wedding. Father was quiet, his anger spent, resigned. He was carefully buttoning his cuffs with some gold links. Mother was already dressed, looking sad and beautiful in a white saree with a blue border. A wicker box with pieces of *kiributh*, *kevun* and *kokis* stood near the front door and she was looking at it uncertainly. Was there any use, she seemed to ask herself, of taking this to a registry office in far off Colombo, a cold bleak place where my son will marry a girl we have never seen and go away from our lives? Suddenly she called out to Podi in the kitchen and told her to take it away.

Why are you in a white saree, *Akka*, wear the pink *Manipuri*, after all it is a wedding, no? It was my aunt talking in one breath as she stepped in through the rear door wiping the mud of the fields from her bare feet on the coir rug.

Mother hastily changed her saree and put on a gold chain round her neck.

What does it matter what you wear, you are not the bride, father said making a feeble attempt at a joke. No one even smiled.

We will be back late. Look after the little ones, mother said to Podi, stepping into the car near the steps. Father sat in front and looked straight ahead. The car glided down the hill like a great black beetle. A wisp of smoke trailed after it and we stood on the steps and watched mother and father go to the wedding.

So, you are not going to your big brother's wedding? They are not taking you because you are not fair and pretty . . . that's why they are not taking you . . . see, your mother is going and she is leaving you behind. Now they will eat cake and ice cream and sweets and you won't get anything . . . what a shame and the first wedding in the family and you are missing everything!

Everyone laughed. It was so funny. They were having such a good time. Even my aunt who had wept so much earlier that day because she could not see this dear nephew at his wedding! Even she. The voices went on, and on.

It seems she has a lot of money, they started in

whispers now, looking covertly towards me. She is the only child in the family and the father has died long ago leaving everything to her. She has lakhs of rupees, they say, and houses in Colombo and estates and all sorts of things. But they are from the South, no? Not a good caste, though they have lots of property, paddy fields and land and houses in their village . . .

His karma to gave gone and passed all those exams and gone to that university or something to meet a girl like that, said the grand-aunt whose sons were morons and could not make it even to the government school.

There was a pall of gloom when these chattering magpies went to their respective homes. Everything was so quiet. I thought of all my golden moments lost to me. This was the time I would watch my mother milk the russet brown cow with the lovely gentle eyes, the milk streaming from her overburdened udders into the white jug, making that squeaky sound which always made me laugh, my mother's gentle hands stroking the smooth flank and the tiny calf with is spindly legs staggering up to his mother's now overflowing udder and sucking, sucking, sucking.

I lay on the floor of the lonely verandah where the old armchair looked desolate without its usual occupant, reading out bits of news in the *Dinamina* and asking me what words would fit into the crossword, laughing at my eagerness to fill in the white squares any old how!

I watched the sun come up above the coconut trees and knew it was time for the walk to the well in grand-aunt's garden close to the paddy land, but today I did not want to go to the well and did not want Podi to swish the water on my thin naked body and lather my hair into a frothy souffle, full of sweet smelling soap, my mother's soap. I wanted my mother, my mother.

The day would end soon, and there would be talk of the wedding and everything would be right again.

I listened to the sound of the car and willed it to come up the hill and stop at the steps and come now, this minute and make everything right again, and take my loneliness away.

That night father went to bed without his dinner. This time there was not going to be a description of the trip to Colombo, the wedding, what they had seen and brought for us and where they had gone. Not this time. We lived all of father's trips every time he went out of the village even for one day, during his after dinner recounting. We knew all about the shops in Colombo, where he bought sweets, bookshops from where he bought us books and the clothes stores from where he bought sarees for my mother and big sister. We had never seen any of these, but he had this knack of making them come alive to us through his trips. Or he would tell us other things, of the world, of wars in other lands, why some people believed some things and others did not and he would make a point with his thumbnail on the tablecloth.

But not tonight. I crept close to my mother. She made room for me on her bed, sighed and put an arm round me. Everything was right again for me. There was no more loneliness, no wedding, no gossip now.

But we did not sleep. Mother's eyes were wide open. Several times she sighed and murmured something, half asleep. The wedding. It was the wedding that would not let her sleep.

'We'll have a big party when he brings the bride home . . . ask all the neighbours and relations,' she once said from nowhere and then I fell asleep, cocooned in my mother's warmth, on the night of the wedding.

Wedding in the Family

*

Next morning the wedding was completely forgotten. Grandmother had died the previous night at her youngest son's house in Moratuwa. The funeral was to be at our house, father being her eldest son. The body was brought home that morning.

Everything quickened and came alive. People crowded into the house and there was plenty of hustle and bustle and the house took on quite a festive air. The gardens were swept and cleaned, the front lawn trimmed, the leaves and grass making a huge bonfire down the hill. Half a mile away a pyre was being built on the cinnamon land and people were constantly coming and going with white paper, steamers and strings, *gok kola* decorations. It was getting terribly exciting.

A tent was put up hastily in the back yard and huge pans were taken down from the smoke blackened shelves over the fireplace and cooking started early that day. Bundles of cinnamon sticks made fragrant fires. Women were bent over cauldrons, sweat streaming down their faces, stirring with huge ladles. In the kitchen Podi was in her element, making tea, laughing with her friends from the village, flirting with the young fellows making the funeral decorations. Excitement was high.

And then the cousins came in droves. The aunts wept by the bier placed in our living room, huge candles lighting up grandmother's weary and lined faces, weary and lined with nearly a century of living and now, even in death, the lines stood out. But the ruffles on her jacket were crisp and the pearls round her neck gleamed.

Father was back to his old self, after the gloom of the wedding. He ordered the men about and scolded the aunts for wasting their time weeping when there was so much to be done. He shooed us out to play and we rolled on the sand, so many cousins together and shouted and laughed. So much excitement, such fun, such a difference to the day before, such a lovely day after the loneliness of the wedding.

Was it only yesterday?

THE MAN THEY CALLED SMALL-BOY

He was three months short of ninety when he died. He passed away as quietly as a leaf falling off a tree. People had come to believe that that was how he would die—as if he'd just opened the back door and slipped away. The event of his death was not one that would be marked by any unusual excitement, they said. It would be as if a man they had seen around a long time, took his departure, unexpectedly, one day, leaving one abode for another in some unknown place and disappearing, never to be heard of again.

It all began, one day, a long, long time earlier, when this man, who had been wandering around, in the streets of Colombo, met a man called Alagu Maniampillai. It was an entirely accidental meeting that took place, at a time when Maniampillai was just starting out to be a businessman.

The two men were quite youthful then. Eventually, it appeared, they hailed from the same country, and after their first meeting they decided that they should continue to meet, which they did, whenever the opportunity arose.

One day Maniampillai asked the other if he would like to be his domestic aid, an offer which the other young man accepted, having nothing else to do except loaf around the streets, looking for the odd job.

Maniampillai was not quite the kind of man one would associate with the world of commerce, a quite unimpressive little man who didn't seem capable of doing anything for himself, but that is what he made himself out to be—a businessman. He had started out, he said, with only a capital of one thousand rupees, just one thousand rupees and nothing more, and this sum he had doubled and trebled in a short time, and he was determined to be the best businessman there was around, and this is what he became—one of the best in the local trade circles in Colombo. It was, it seemed, a remarkable achievement for so small a man, with so small a claim on people's attention. He was barely five feet tall, but for some odd reason people always him a second look. First, he was a very dark man, and he had a head like the dome of a church, completely round, with his hair cropped very short, and then there was this pair of sharp, calculating eyes under his heavy brows, which bored into people, sometimes with a shrewd glint in them and sometimes with even a bit of menace.

Alagu Maniampillai, at the beginning of the relationship with his factotum, decided he would put the young fellow in his place, and for a start called him Podian so he wouldn't get any fancy ideas about himself. The word Podian had come to mean any number of things and came, in the end, to mean nothing at all. Podian meant small boy; it also meant a fellow of no consequence, a nondescript, a houseboy, or anything else one intended it to mean, and Podian the young man became, and Podian he stayed for the rest of his days. It was the only name he knew and responded to. That was the beginning of it all.

Alagu forged ahead, expanding his business ventures. He was relentless in his pursuits. He added shipping and export to his other activities. Along the way, he purchased land and became a land owner as well. He was teaching himself the business methods of the colonial rulers. They did business on the one hand and grabbed land on the other. He decided if that was good enough for them it was good enough for him. He observed the colonial masters very closely and carried out their methods with meticulous care.

He would, sometimes, return home at dusk from having supervised the loading of a cargo of copra and spices with a feeling of fulfilment; at other times he would stand on the sea shore and watch a ship take off into the setting sun, and, watching it go, he would tell himself that it was his stuff going where all trade goods went at the time. It would give him a great feeling of fulfilment. He was no ordinary man, he told himself.

In later years, he would try to recreate a picture of the old days. Alagu and Podian were old men then, in the twilight of their lives—they would sit together and talk of the times when the shipping firms were the hub of life in the commercial world of Colombo, the old harbour full of ships, feverishly being loaded and unloaded, with spices, tea, rubber and copra for the outward journey, and manufactured goods, from England, coming back in them on the return journey. The harbour was alive with barges, launches, tugs, junks, Doneys and even quaint little ships with sails and masts and rigging like they had in the pirate ships that sailed the Caribbean seas. It seemed like a fairy tale to Podian.

Those were the days, Alagu would remind Podian; 'Men were men then, not little grey monkeys chiti-chittering up on the trees, little grey monkeys, having all kinds of fancy ideas about themselves.' Alagu would think back to those times, so full of reminiscences, of dainty ladies tripping along the shopping arcade, past the shops, in their long skirts which they would lift up delicately and sweep round their ankles, with their gloved hands, while further on, a pith-hatted gentleman would emerge from one of the big shops with a lackey carrying his purchases for him.

The story of Podian began in an extraordinary fashion it seemed, a long time before he met Alagu Maniampillai in a Colombo street. He appeared, he said, one day, on the northern shores of the island, having slipped over from India in a flat-bottomed boat, along with a group of other adventurous young men. After several adventures of a dubious nature, Podian had, finally, surfaced in Colombo, a place that immediately went to his head like hot toddy. He couldn't get over the things he saw— motor cars chugging up and down, rickshaws flying along, with 'coolies' pulling them in place of bulls and horses; tram cars rumbling and clanging along steel rails, along the elegant highway of York Street, and alongside them, horse carriages moving sedately by, with fashionable ladies riding in them. This was a sight worth seeing, he thought, standing awestricken on the side of the road, a stripling of about eighteen or nineteen.

He was so full of wonder and excitement that he forgot, for the moment, how he had come here, an alien in a foreign land, with no documents of any kind. The moment a black-uniformed policeman appeared he would slip away and stay undercover, until he felt safe enough to reappear again. It seemed a bit strange to him that, although Ceylon and India were closely linked as colonies of the British, one needed these scraps of paper or documents or whatever you called them. He hadn't a clue as to what they were meant to be, but it seemed one had to have these things or you had no right to be here or even exist. You were just nothing, a phantom. He decided, in one of his brighter moments, that if one was only a phantom, with no visible or tangible existence he then, had no need of documents either. He could just disappear if things got hot and then reappear.

After he had attached himself to Alagu Maniampillai, he suddenly discovered that all he had to do to get rid of the official difficulties, of the kind they had been talking about, was to tell his master, and he fixed it at once. He would wave the thing away as if by a magic wand. No one knew how, but the obstacles would disappear.

Alagu, a minority man himself, a descendant of a migrant from India from more distant times than Podian, realized by then that he had, quite by accident, come upon a serving man who suited his needs to perfection— a man who had no personal documents of any kind whatsoever, totally stateless, and, therefore, entirely dependent on him. He could entrust the management of his bachelor establishment to such a man, while he went about exploring the possibilities of the world of commerce and business.

Podian, on the other hand, decided to make the most of the world he had been thrust into. He was wise enough to realize that he was bound to his master by the absence of valid documents of residence; he was an illicit immigrant, but that very shortcoming he was going to turn to his advantage. He would win his master's trust, and through that trust, bind his master to him. There were ways of doing this; he would become the trusted link between Alagu and his household which had grown recently. There was a cook, a second servant, a gardener, and, more recently, a driver had been added, when Alagu bought himself a car.

Alagu was too busy to bother about what went on in his household. All he wanted was order which he could return to after a hard day, getting his shipments loaded, and the local buying completed. The chap, Podian, appeared to be keeping everything under control.

The servants, all local men, didn't appear to resent being ordered about by Podian; well, that was all right—that's how he wanted it. Then, one day, he had a rude awakening . . . his factotum had a place for him too in his scheme of things.

'You've still not had your shave this morning,' barked Podian at him, that morning, with a suddenness that took the wind out of him; 'you keep sitting around, and I keep marching up and down, waiting for you to be ready. It this the way to do things—you a big business *dorai*? Haven't I enough trouble trying to keep this household together? What would become of it if I sat around too?'

Alagu was flummoxed. He sat there staring at Podian as if he had been struck by a flying missile. He couldn't believe it had happened. He recovered soon enough, and leaping up he yelled back. 'You foul-mouthed tree toad, you scavenging black crow, you . . . you . . . already starting to give me your back-talk . . . you . . . you . . . good for nothing . . .', Alagu was livid with rage.

'All right, if that's how you want it?' said Podian indignantly, hurling the duster away, 'I'll quit today—you just tell me and I'll quit.'

'You're quitting today, are you, you fool?' scoffed Alagu.

'Yes—what's more, I am doing it right now.'

'And where the hell are you going after that?'

'I'll go anywhere; I'll walk the streets; I'll go back to India; I'll find a bigger man to work for. India is a large enough place, with a lot more fish in it.'

'You're going to swim the Palk Strait, are you? You're going to cross it on a raft? How else can you enter India? They wouldn't know whether you're a goat or a donkey, with no documents to prove who you are. You'll be back in the sea as fast as you land there.'

'I can get back there the same way I came here—can't I?'

'All right, all right, cut the cackle; come and get this shaving done. I've things to do. I can't waste a morning arguing with a half-witted tree toad,' said Alagu, watching Podian shrewdly, and thinking there was quite a bit more gumption in the stateless castaway than he suspected.

He had a sudden, secret regard for the fellow, a minority man like himself, but a man who was ready to give life a fight on his terms.

So Podian brought the shaving things together, thrust his master into his couch, lathered him savagely, and shaved him with such quick, sharp strokes that it frightened Alagu into thinking the idiot was going to slit his throat. Podian, next, went about laying out Alagu's clothes with the same brusque, ill-tempered manner, and, like a gust of breeze, he darted about the room, spreading the china-silk shirt, gold tie-pin, finely woven tussore trousers and coat and black shoes. The black shoes were polished like glass. Polishing shoes and sandals was a mania Podian had acquired. He was accustomed to polishing his own sandals with the greatest care, but these were London-made shoes, and they needed the extra rub or two; they needed it more than even the sandals he wore to his morning prayers at the nearby Hindu temple.

This, however, was not the only sort of fight they had, in those early days. They fought about a host of things, the trivial and the not so trivial, their voices raised, their tempers roused. The fights, you would think, ought to have led to estrangement, anger and enmity; at least to ill-feeling and bitterness, but not in their case. On the contrary, they appeared to thrive on these fights. Alagu found this was good training for his encounters in the business field, and for terrorizing his subordinates in his office, and Podian found it an excellent means of instilling terror into the other servants. Anyone who could fight the headstrong, truculent Alagu Maniampillai, in the way he did was, certainly, no ordinary man. In Podian's case, it was consciously directed and manoeuvred so it would intimidate the servants. Alagu didn't quite cotton onto it at the beginning, and thinking the fellow was really serious about wanting order in the house, he fell into line and accepted the routine Podian set even for him. Alagu liked efficiency in the conduct of any kind of undertaking. He was convinced that this was the secret of the success of his white mentors.

'Routine, old chap, routine—it's what made the British Empire into what it is,' said one of the colonial businessmen, a man called Meyerside whom Alagu particularly admired. Following Meyerside's advice, he got things running in his office with a rare kind of order and efficiency. Not a squeak came from any of his assistants or clerks. He was a tyrant, despite his diminutive size—the self charging, self-propelling dynamo who appeared to have got his organization running on his own system of dynamics and motion. Alagu Maniampillai's business world expanded; so did his household. Silver-plated cigarette boxes, beautifully-framed pictures on the wall, and a piano in the sitting room, all appeared, as if magically. He didn't know one key from another on the piano key-board. He purchased great leather-bound books, which, strangely, he even attempted to read. All these were displayed prominently so his business associates would see he was not just paying lip-service to their social habits. He treated his friends lavishly—gave them a choice of different brands of British whiskies, brandies and gin, and to give a demonstration of his expanding tastes, he pushed in a bit of French wine and Dutch cheese along with them, but he was shrewd enough to realize the British liked to see their own produce around the place. Sometimes, he tried to outdo them in the lavishness and the complications of the white man's eating rituals. He began to carve up entire turkeys at the dinner table and spread out a whole range of cutlery and crockery. Earlier, he had been completely happy eating with his fingers and winding up his meal with a chew of betel, the aromatic and antiseptic leaf that he had so enjoyed in the past. He had discovered that the white community thought this was a barbarous habit. Although his instincts told him that his was much less harmful than getting drunk on whisky and becoming dizzy with tobacco smoke.

So he dropped the habit of chewing betel as quickly as he dropped his sarong to replace it with the quite inconvenient pyjamas. He had also learned that it was the white man's custom to finish a meal with liqueurs, cigars and coffee. He immediately gave instructions to Podian that was how it was to be in his household as well.

One day, Alagu Maniampillai was complimented on the way he wore his bow-tie.

'You can always recognize a gentleman by the way he wears his bow tie,' said a friend, a man called Algie Bastow, a tea planter. 'You take that tie off Alagu Pillai and show me how you do it, and I'll tell you whether you're a gentleman or not.' Alagu promptly pulled off his tie and did it up again, in a flash. 'Excellent,' cried Algie Bastow, 'Excellent, Alagu. You've, certainly, got the makings of a gentleman—these days when your business has expanded a bit more, maybe, I'll recommend you to be admitted as guest at our club.'

Alagu was beaming with pleasure. For a moment he had feared he'd slip up on the damn thing; but it had gone off without a hitch. Even Podian, who had watched the scene from a distance, a bit amused at the childish games his superiors played, had momentary fear for his master, and was pleased when he carried it off to the delight of the colonial master.

Podian was now his master's accomplished factotum, bowing to the visitors, fetching for them, and they, in turn, tipped him lavishly; they did it with a flourish. It enlarged their image and gave them a great feeling of self-satisfaction, and Podian, dressed in his white tunic coat and snow white *vertie*, served his master's friends, faultlessly, bowing as low as his tunic coat permitted him. Of all his master's visitors, however, there was one Podian liked the best of all. He was a man called Jerry Buckskin whose natural warmth and friendliness Podian took to in a quite unexpected fashion.

One day, Jerry Buckskin had confessed to Alagu, in Podian's presence, that he 'ad been joost an ordinary man in London, but bettin' on th'orses he made enuff dough to cumava; it 'ad ben toch-an-go fura-while, but evenchooly he'd got a job as an assistant in one of the shippin' firms, an' he'd made it 'ere, an' he loikit 'era.'

The confession had impressed Podian. It was not often a colonial master made a confession of that nature. Podian got on well with Buckskin. They got on so well that Buckskin decided he'd teach Podian some English, and stumbling and stuttering, Podian learned a bit here and a bit there. It was easier learning it from Jerry than from some of the others who seemed to speak a different and more difficult kind of English.

'You're a good fellow, Podian,' said Jerry to him one day. 'I loika simpal fellow but who 'as a good 'art—none of th'airs loik some the fellas from mi' country give. Oh, I'd sae tha'gits mi' blud boilin. They got no hea' nor 'art—only the bludy airs. Ere's a hundred rupees from mi' boy; it's a gift—yea, cross mi'art—it's gift-taekit man, taekit'.

'Velly march you thank you, velly march you thank

you,' said Podian, accepting the gift gratefully as from one friend to another.

'I loik a simpal fella loik tha'guy—I tell yur,' said Jerry to Alagu. Jerry patted his stomach saying it. 'News he got to get on in life, but you don't reely trick 'im—not the airs sumtha fellas from mi' country 'era—no, thaai down't taek'im. He kowtows ole right, but inside he knows it's all just a lota stuffin' there's in 'em-yea, Alagu, yea taekit from mi', he's not fooled.' Alagu roared with laughter. 'That fellow I picked up fraamg dha zreet—no edugashun, nothing—zarp all right, but nothing more—just Podian. I call him Podian—that's all he is. I kick him into zreet tomorrow, and he'll be taken and throang into the sea—where he cumfraa.' 'But yea taekit from mi' Alagu, ole boy—he's got sumthing in im; he's got sumthin in 'im ole right; I feel it right 'ere, in mi' belly, inside 'ere. He's deep 'un, ole roit- no mistakin.'

Podian, in the meanwhile, matured and developed in several unexpected directions. His lean, hawk-like ebony face even began to take on predatory characteristics, like that of the serpent eagle. His master had got on in the world, but that didn't mean he had no right to his own preferences from among the colonial masters who called at the house. He and his master, Alagu, sometimes, would have violent quarrels over what Podian considered the unfair way Alagu treated Jerry Buckskin. He insisted that his Master Maniampillai treated Master Buckskin in a somewhat indifferent manner—it was sometimes even shabby. For one thing the glasses were not the best, not the crystal ones he brought out for some of the others. He, certainly, didn't bring the crystal glasses for Buckskin Master, and that, Podian said, was not playing fair. Podian didn't like different standards being applied for the white man he considered his friend. What was even worse, thought Podian, was that his *dorai* fetched only the cheaper whiskies for him, in the half empty bottles, and that, said Podian, was mean.

'You two-headed black crow—you trying to tell me how I am to treat my visitors. You're getting too big for your sandals, you scavenging black crow, you unwashed, dirty *kallathoni*,' yelled Alagu, unexpectedly referring to Podian's statelessness—*kallathoni* being the local term for illicit immigrant. Podian's face had darkened at the reference, but he decided he'd ignore it. It touched a very sore spot inside him, but he let it pass. He, however, wouldn't yield on the point of his *dorai's* bad manners.

'You don't insult a visitor to your home—not in the poorest village do you do it,' he said.

He went on then to elaborate on it. He himself never took but the purest flowers and sandalwood sticks as offerings to God Shiva. This was a lesson he had learned from an uncle, the priest of the temple in his village in India, who had once kicked him out of the temple for making an offering of some stale flowers. 'You're not cheating God Shiva—you're cheating yourself. You do that often enough and you'll go rotten inside you,' his uncle, had shouted at him.

Then there came this time of great change. The World War brought about unprecedented changes. Europe was in shambles. England itself was in great economic trouble. People were on the move, and the European community on the island, uncertain of their future, began to leave for home, and there were rumblings of change in India and Ceylon as well. It was this that brought on wrinkles of worry on Podian's eagle face, but he kept calm and went about his work, trying to disguise his fears. He was, however, a troubled man. His uncle, the priest, had taught him the Vedas, and even demonstrated methods of meditation practised by the ancients. Podian, however, in his search for adventure, had shed all that, but some of the things he had learned as a boy, seemed, once more, to stir mysteriously inside him. It seemed to bring him in touch with hidden resources within him, resources he had never thought he had.

One day, Jerry Buckskin came along looking more despondent than he had been in a long time.

'Well, Podian,' he said in his gritty, drawling voice; 'the fat's in th'fire for mi' ole boy. I'll be packin' mi' bags the beatin' it off this 'ere beautiful shores and waeving palm trees and noice people.'

'*Enna Dorai, enna idi?*' asked the puzzled Podian from his Master, suddenly, lapsing into Tamil, turning from Jerry Buckskin to his Master and then back to Jerry Buckskin again, visibly disturbed. The old man Alagu Maniampillai, a bit slower now, with age creeping on, made no comment. He just nodded his head. Everything had to change—they come, they go—it was the way in the gamble. He was used to it. His was a businessman's reaction. If a man brought him business he treated him accordingly; if the business stopped he dropped him. Jerry was going, that's all there was to it. He'll make other friends and carry on as best as he could. 'Blimey, ole boy, can't he understand the Brits are pullin outa 'ere—going back to ole blighty they're and we fellas gotta go somewhere a bloke can pick up some dough and go'on livin' and even, maybe, finda foin lassy whose lap I can lay mi' 'ead on—it's ole I'm askin'—note mooch, is it?'

Jerry's going was the first great blow to Podian. This was the first bit of tangible evidence that changes were going on that were bigger than he realized. Finally, the British left the island. They handed it back to the inhabitants. Ceylon was independent, and the new government began to take stock of what she had to govern—twenty five thousand square miles of land, with nearly ten or eleven million people living in it, besides, something close on half a million Indian labourers, with no proper status either in Ceylon or India, to be accounted for; what was more—a fair number of them were illicit immigrants.

Podian wandered about shaken by the events that appeared suddenly to crowd in on him. The going of Jerry had affected him more deeply than was apparent. There had been something of a kindred spirit in the two men. Jerry, though a Britisher, was in spirit a man without anywhere. He was, like Podian now, a wanderer, a wayfarer, stopping for a while in a place and moving on again. Life had no permanancy; why should one have a permanent home. Nothing, according to Jerry, had any permanency. You met a man in the street one moment and then you parted, maybe, for ever. What's the point of being anybody, being a nabob, a pukka sahib if one is here for a moment and gone forever the next. 'In the end what did it all come to—a bit or 'orse dung dryin' tha'sun—what difference between you rotting six feet down and that bit of orse-dung. The fellas 'ad tha' sense 'ere to . . . . what's the word . . . cri . . . cri . . . maet— that's it—crimaete, burn you down to th'ashus—you're reduced o nothin'. Naw, looata fella loik Podian—no blood pressure, no twisted bones or anythin' loik that, and hon awelled do yer think he's . . . comin' onto seventy five or eighty—if he was a day, oi bet, and moind yer, yet he walks on his 'is aun two feet and use 'is aun two 'ands, reads the paepus, no glasses, moind yer. I tell yer Alagu, that's the sorta life fa mi'—sumwhere there's no big nabob goin' throwin' is weight arund.'

Then followed the discussions that took place between the governments of India and Ceylon over the repatriation of Indian nationals of recent origin, or anyone else without valid documents of residence. Podian pretended he knew nothing about all this. The exercise of repatriation would, no doubt, be spread over a long period of time. This sort of thing couldn't be done in a hurry; but, to his great misfortune, the process was speeded up for some reason Podian couldn't fathom. They smoked out illicit immigrants from all sorts of obscure places and hideouts. Podian rode the storm like a petrel, and, to all appearances, he was indifferent to the operation. He behaved as if the entire activity was an act of gargantuan folly perpetrated by a bunch of men who had become deranged. He had a curious innocence of governmental and administrative matters, and it was this innocence that gave him immunity. He dismissed the whole idea of return as not being worth a moment's thought. How were they going to prove he was or was not a citizen of the country? He was going to stay put and no one was going to budge him an inch. Besides, he had become accustomed to this way of life in the country, and he, like his Master, had advanced in years. His Master, it was true, had grown a bit dotty with the years going by. He was making impossible demands of people. He wanted people to roll back the world, bring back the old times, and give it reality. He would come to dinner, all dressed up in dinner jacket and bow-tie. He demanded that they too came down to dinner all dressed up just as in the British times, and underneath his jacket, forgetfully, wore his sarong, sometimes. What was more—he would invite non-existent people to dinner. He had got so cranky that he would sometimes yell at Podian for not getting dressed up for the visitors he was expecting.

Podian had his sleeping quarters in an enclosed wooden cubicle, built onto a storeroom of what was an outhouse. This was his den; he turned half of it into a shrine room, on the walls of which he plastered pictures of the goddess Parvathi, of Ganesh, of Krishna, and a couple of other gods from the Hindu pantheon. In between the gods he had, as if it were for good luck, pushed in a photograph of the King of England, and, also, smuggled into another vacant spot the picture of the

Pope. The Pope was a concession he had granted his Master, who was a Catholic. Podian did not want to take chances with those who had been his protectors. Over some of the pictures he had hung garlands of long-faded flowers, some of which were crumbling into dust, but remained held together by bits of thread and dried-up stem as if by some mysterious spiritual power.

Each morning and evening he would climb the flight of steps into his den and he would light a candle and a couple of incense sticks. Then, he would strip himself to the waist, his thin, black body like a bronze figure of an eagle about to take flight, his hands lifted over his head like plucked wings, and, poised there, he would slowly pivot round, muttering his ancient Sanskrit prayers, and whatever else he remembered of the Vedic scriptures and the Bhagavadgita. He would pivot round for several minutes, his thin, black throat pumping to the rhythm of the words. In his mind, perhaps, he saw these gods and the long dead British King, whose picture was on his wall, and even the Pope, take form and shape, and stand round him in a protective ring. Gods were not like men—nor were kings—they didn't abandon those who were faithful to them.

However, it seemed as if he had resigned himself to the unassailable fact that the past was gone. He decided to accept whatever new conditions life offered him; yet, what was there for an old man to do back in India, except ask for handouts. It was no good. That was no way out. He remembered something Jerry had once said—true, he was drunk at the time—but there was reason in what he had said. All human beings, he had said, came from a few hairy men that looked, at the beginning, like gorillas and chimpanzees. Both he and his Master had laughed at the idea. Jerry had insisted it was true; the scientists had said so, he had cried. He, drunkenly and vehemently, had insisted it was true.

Podian, retreating to his den, thought of this. He remembered how vehemently Jerry insisted on it. It had to have some truth for him to have got so worked up when he was doubted. One couldn't be sure about these things—the scientists, they wouldn't go around saying things if they weren't true. The Vedas said more or less the same thing. All things emerged from Brahma and all things, in the end, went back to Brahma. So, why could it not be true that, at the beginning, all mankind began from one source. There was this other thing Jerry had said about the Buddhists that had got Podian thinking now. Jerry had said that the Buddhist belief was that nothing was permanent. All things, according to them, were in a state of constant change. Podian had asked the other servants if this was true. 'Yes,' they had said, '*Annicavaka sankhara uppada vaya dhammino*' meant that all component things came into being, decayed and passed into nothingness. Difficult ideas, these were, but it made him think. All these ideas were suddenly flooding his mind. They came clearly through—the words forming clear patterns in his brain. He was not capable of sustained thinking, but, suddenly, it seemed as if the difficulties of the kind that have been obstacles to ordinary men seemed to disappear. He was able, suddenly, to make clear patterns of thought from sentences recalled from the past. It all seemed to come flooding back, and these thought patterns began to recur in a strange manner.

In another sense, Podian seemed to be acquiring the kind of innocence that children and sages had in common, which gave them capacity to believe in the incredible and bridge gaps in logical thinking. He was willing now to give any idea a chance if it was helping him overcome the present fears. The only moment these fears returned was when his brother, who was still alive in India, started to write, urging him to return to India.

'Come back, you fool—that's no place for you now,'

he wrote. 'How can I come back? Do you think I can swim the sea and creep into India? I need a passport. I need documents.'

'Passport—is that your big worry? You should have told me. I can get a passport. Don't worry, I'll fix it. Till you get your photographs and other papers, I'll send you mine.'

He promptly went and got himself a passport, and carefully wrapping it in several layers of brown paper, sent it to Podian. When Podian opened the packet and saw it was his brother's passport that had come in it he felt a great sadness come over him.

'You show them this and say it is your brother's. Also show them this letter I've sent, and the old photograph of our family. That will prove you belong here.'

Podian's brother, a wise man in other matters of life—he knew the Vedas and the Bhaghavadgita by heart, and, at one stage, had even studied folk medicine, was as innocent as a child in these administrative matters. He couldn't believe that they had divided up the world and its people, and that obstructions of this nature could be put in the way of anyone whose desire was simply to return to his own country, which any man had a right to. It was incredible that the world could go so completely crazy to deny a man his right to go back home.

Podian, for his part, began to have bad dreams. They soon turned into nightmares. He would wake up screaming for help, and, afterwards, he would find himself lying there, trembling. He had never had dreams of this kind before—all those people running, swarms of them running after him, shouting and yelling.

*

'*Kallathoni*,' they cried, '*Kallathoni*'.

And he kept running, his legs giving way under him, and he trying to run, and the sea he was running towards receding, and there was the crowd, gaining on him until he finally fell on his knees, pleading for mercy. 'No, no, I am an old man—I'll be dead soon. I cannot run anymore, please, please, spare me.'

They were frightful dreams that got him worried. So, at last, he decided he would seek help. He went to a friend and asked him how he could set about going back to his country. 'Oh, that's simple. There's a friend of mine who will fix it for a sum of money. It's all fixed—that's the way it's done.'

'Is there no other way—no law? I am too old to go to jail, doing illegal things.'

'Don't be a fool. You don't go to jail. You just give this man some money and he fixes it. What laws are you talking about? There are no laws—not in this sort of thing—it's all fixed.'

'If I just go to the police and say I am a *kallathoni* will they send me back home, you think? There was this Englishman—he was my master's friend—he said, in his country, you just went along and said you were an Englishman and you wanted a passport, and they gave it to you—maybe they asked questions, but they gave it to you.'

'It's not so simple—you've got it all wrong. First, you are just Podian—you have no other name. They'll ask you for your other names, and you have none—you don't remember any. Then, they'll ask where you were born; right, you know that—they'll say how do you prove it. They'll ask you a lot of other questions. You see, they want to get rid of you—you're creating problems for them—officials don't like problems they can't solve. So, you just go along and fix it, or you butter up some official—it's the way it's done here. The laws, you're crazy to talk of laws—they're just barriers they fix to keep fellows like you and me outside so that the big shots can come and go as they please.'

James Goonewardene

One night, then, a thief stole into Podian's den, when Podian was asleep, and took his razor, along with the best sarong he had, the one he wore to go to the *kovil*. The Zen Buddhists say that enlightenment or what they call Satori, comes suddenly, in a flash. The theft of the razor was the event that brought the final flash of truth to Podian. It took him a long time to reconcile himself to the loss of his razor. The loss of the sarong was a different matter. The loss of the razor snapped the cord that linked him to his whole past; the loss became symbolic to him. He remembered that it was Jerry who gave him this razor, a gift he cherished very much, and, now it was gone. This had to mean something, he thought to himself, or why should the thief have taken the razor of all the things that were in his room. He pondered on he thing; he rolled it over in his mind, and the more he did so the more the thing acquired this symbolic character; the past and all the things associated with it were being stripped away from him, and he was being left naked, naked and exposed to the world's jibes, its lack of coherence, its madness, and he was reaching the point when he was not going to fight any of it—not anymore. Surrender was much easier.

The other servants said he should get himself a safety razor. He scoffed at the idea. He had never had any faith in modern gadgets. He saw the terrible things that modern inventions could do—death from motor car accidents, trains, aeroplanes, the dropping of bombs and the firing of guns, facts that became more and more insistent and widespread and demonstrative of man's irrationality and madness, the madness of men who pinned their faith in mechanical things. No, he would not buy himself a safety razor. He would just let his beard grow instead. It seemed like an ordinary decision a man makes. There were these changes going on inside his mind, and this was a reflection of those changes. These external changes, how they

The Man They Called Small-Boy

came about and caused these changes in his life style were strange, imperceptible things. He began then to stay up in his den for longer periods—sitting in a lotus pose. Meditating in the way his uncle, the priest, used to sit when meditating. The periods of silence and meditation would stretch out as time went. He would come down only to take his daily bath or meals. He had always been particular about the cleanliness of his body and clothes.

For a long while now he had given up his habit of praying, standing in front of his pictures, those of the different gods and the British King and the Pope, the ones on which he had garlands of faded flowers hanging. He did not stand in front of them and pray anymore. He had dropped the habit. The pictures were still up there, on the walls, but he ignored them now. He stopped deceiving himself about the mysterious powers there were in them. He did not even glance in their direction.

One day, then, he did an even stranger thing. He went round taking the pictures down. There were empty spaces up on the walls with years of dust clinging to them. He cleaned all this now. He wiped the walls clean. He took all the pictures and tossed them all into the rubbish bin. He merely glanced at the servants who had gathered to see him do this. They said nothing. They merely stood there and gazed with amazement. Their stares did not bother him. He went on and having completed his task he returned to his den, and the servants would, thereafter, creep up to take a peep at him, and there he would be seated, meditating.

His master Alagu Maniampillai, also very old now, was lying paralyzed, half deaf and nearly blind, but alive. There was only his body performing its reflexes and nervous functions, excreting and continuing to live. Podian would go and look at his master, lying there on his bed, but his face did not reflect the thoughts that went on in his mind. He was shedding all his links with the world.

It was not his master lying there now. That person was gone. He seemed to have reconciled himself to the fact.

Podian continued to perform his meditations, and was now taking only one meal a day. He seemed, in some strange fashion, to be reaching some kind of inner illumination, for his face, still eagle-like, had taken on a more settled and calmer aspect. His face, sometimes, even seemed to glow, his lips relaxed in that smile that one is supposed to see on the faces of people who had made their peace with god or reached a state of enlightenment, *samadhi* or *satori*, or whatever the particular culture called that state of peace. Nothing seemed to disturb him, the servants whispering, the thud of their feet, their movement to and fro. He was beyond their reach, and even when he came out of his deep silence, he was no longer the man they used to know and think of as a fellow servant. He was beyond all that.

One morning they took him his glass of milk as on other mornings, but he was lying in his cot as if still asleep.

He was dead. The servants then banded together, decked him out in his coffin, in his best clothes, his silk chemise and *verti*, and put round his neck a green, striped shawl. His head and face were cleanly shaven. He looked like a bronze sculpture of some priest they had dug up from some ancient temple. Even in death he was something apart.

The Brahmin priest chanting the ancient Sanskrit word transferred the fire from the brass vessel to the clay vessel, and then back again, while he threw into them a variety of substances that crackled and burnt and gave up a fine fragrance, and into this fire he threw other substances that were supposed to represent the components of the human body. This way they believed they were purging Podian's body of any impurities that still remained. So they prepared it for the final burning, the cremation. This, in some strange fashion, seemed to the servants a bit meaningless. This was only the shell. Where was the man who had occupied it, and had been its resident for nearly ninety years? But they went through with it because this was the way the living fulfilled their duty by the dead.

The next day, they took his ashes and immersed them in the Indian ocean, the same sea that washed the shores of not only India, but Sri Lanka and Africa as well. So, he merged with Brahma, and there were no laws now to contain him in this country or that. He needed no passports or documents of any kind. He had triumphed over all that. There was, however, the mystery of his death. It seemed, in some strange way, he had willed it at the last moment. He had no organic disease of any kind, just the eczema which had troubled him, but that too had disappeared, it seemed, in the last stages. Yet, in the way he had settled himself in his cot, before passing away, it seemed that he had decided the time and place in which to take his departure, and so he went, as mysteriously as the birth and death of stars.

Part Two: Stories from the Sinhalese

Contents

The Torn Coat   107
    Martin Wickremasinghe (1924)

Going Back   113
    Gunadasa Amarasekara (1956)

Sarana   127
    Ediriwira Sarachchandra (1969)

The Cart   162
    Somaratne Balasuriya (1991)

The Torn Coat

'We need a loan of Mr. Edwin's black coat for a day.' The young man seated on the veranda of 'Srinivasa' who said this was between twenty and twenty-four years old. He was not an educated man but had had the kind of instruction that in those days could be acquired at the village school. He had learned his letters there as a child, had begun with the Manual of Buddhism and studied up to the *Anuruddha Satakaya*. 'A mouth that has not recited the *Sakaskada* is an empty anthill' was a saying common among villagers at the time.

He had first learned to write on a sand board at the school house. As a result, even when he wrote on paper his letters were enormous. When writing a letter, even a few sentences in his own hand would fill two or three sheets of large-sized paper.

He was seated now on the edge of his chair, dressed in a sarong, with another thrown over his shoulder. He scratched the edge of the chair nervously, as if to test whether he could scrape it with his fingernail. His face, which had on it a large nose and cheeks like two well-stuffed pillows, had a pair of eyes that revealed a certain timidity, a fear of crowds and a deference to authority.

About sixty years ago, the sarong and banian or under shirt had been the attire of the rich folk in the village. There were no trouser-wearing gentlemen then, unlike now. Only the son of the village headman wore a coat and a tweed cloth. Perhaps the villagers thought a coat suited only a government official and were themselves content to wear a sarong and banian, or a sarong with another flung over one shoulder.

'Ah Cornelis, why do you want a black coat?'

'O wife of the headman, don't you know, it is a wedding,'

'A wedding?'

'Yes.'

'Whose?'

Cornelis smiled but did not answer. The headman's wife, her curiosity roused, kept pressing him but Cornelis remained silent. Finally, guessing the reason behind his silence, the headman's wife winked and said with a half smile, 'So the wedding is yours then?'

'I don't know . . . they say it is for me,' said the youth looking down shyly and scraping the edge of the chair even more vigorously.

'Well, you might have said so! From where is the girl?'

'From the house of Agonis, junior.'

'Then it is a good match. They have plenty of land. I doubt you'll get any cash though. Agonis is an old miser. When do you want the coat?'

'For the day after tomorrow.'

'Ah, Cornelis, should one wear old clothes for an occasion such as this? Your father is not a man without money. Ask your father to have a coat made for you.'

'When I told him I wanted a coat sewn, he scolded me.'

In those days when western ways were not as widespread as now, villagers did not know the price of *lakka* cloth. Some believed that to buy a cloth of *lakka* one needed the equivalent of a piece of land. The headman's wife knew that a black coat was not as expensive as Cornelis' father imagined, but she preferred not to mention it. If people like Cornelis discovered its real price, then her son's black coat would lose its value and, not only that, even the family's status in the village might be affected. So she decided to say nothing more about it.

'Well, yes, you can have it.'

'I would like the tu-weed cloth too.'

'The tw-eed cloth too!' said the headman's wife trying hard to pronounce the English word correctly. She herself knew no English but she had heard her son say the word.

'Yes, also a shirt, a tie, and a pair of shoes. I'll use them carefully and return them.'

'Will Mr. Edwin's shoes fit you?'

'My father says, it will be enough if I can manage in them for the day.'

'In that case, there is no problem.'

*

On the wedding morning Cornelis rose early, and dressed. The coat was a little too small. After pulling and pushing he managed to get the two ends together and buttoned it. The shoes were so big that they fell of when he lifted his foot. He poked two pieces of cloth into them and temporarily adjusted them so that they would stay on for the occasion.

Cornelis was a handsome, well-built young man. His eyes were small. His forehead was not too narrow, his nose was long and sharp, his lips fine and his mouth small. When dressed in a sarong and a banian he looked handsome, a responsible young man. But now decked in the borrowed cloth and coat he looked quite unattractive. His natural fear of social gatherings and crowds had increased a hundredfold after he had dressed himself in the borrowed clothes. Simple Cornelis now looked a congenital idiot. True, he had never been considered a great intellectual, but he had also not been thought a fool.

Though a grown-up, Cornelis was still childlike in his obedience to his parents. Whatever his parents said he believed to be right and true. He had never stepped beyond the limits of his home town. He knew nothing of the wide world and had agreed to get married purely because his parents wished him to.

To accompany the relatives to the bride's house, to perform the marriage rites by tying a chain round the bride's neck and giving gifts, to proceed then to the house of the Registrar of Marriages and repeat all the things he said, and to finally sign his name in the register were all difficult, exhausting and very nearly impossible tasks for Cornelis.

Finally, he escaped the clutches of the Registrar and together with his wife sat down in the horse cart. It was only then that a slight sense of relief came over him. Cornelis had seen his bride only once before. He had never spoken to her. Even now, though she was his wife, she was a total stranger. He saw her cowering in shyness and fear. If he were to so much as say a word he felt sure she would turn on him.

The bridal couple and their entourage reached the groom's house by six that evening.

*

'Why are you sad,' asked Cornelis' wife approaching her husband who was sitting mournfully in a chair. Cornelis'

The Torn Coat

parents had feted the wedding guests. Having feasted, the men and women who had escorted the couple wished them well and left. After they had gone Cornelis had retired to his room and now sat lost in mournful thought. His wife stood beside him leaning a hand against the small table. A quarter of an hour passed but not a word escaped Cornelis' lips. He just sat, an immobile statue. His wife, unable to understand it all, walked slowly up to him and placed her small right hand on his shoulder.

'Why are you sad?' she asked again. She got no answer. Again and again she asked but got no response. Then she knelt before him.

'Oh why are you crying?' she asked in a trembling voice. Her words fell on Cornelis' ear like a chant of grief. He lifted his head and looked at his wife. Seeing her lips trembling, her eyes so full of love and her sweet face wrung with shame, Cornelis felt an emotion he had never experienced before.

'I was not crying. I was thinking.'

'Why do you grieve? I . . . Am I . . . ?'

'No . . .'

It was a relief to her to know that his sadness was not of her making. The doubts and fears that had overtaken her vanished.

'Why are you sad? Tell me.'

'I don't like to say it.'

'No, no, you must tell me.'

Asida's pleading finally made Cornelis reveal the reason behind his grief.

'The cloth and coat I wore tóday were not mine. I borrowed them from a certain person and wore them. Just as we approached your house, when getting down from the cart, the coat caught on a nail and tore. Later, to add to everything, a cigar burned a hole in the cloth. I must now pay compensation for both these items. Your father has given no cash as dowry. My father is upset about that and will never give me the money to pay for those things.'

'We will find a way to pay for them.'

'How will we pay? You don't know my father. All the money I earned is with him. 'Young people don't need money,' he says and takes it all. It is only with the greatest reluctance that he gives me my expenses even for food and clothes. My father will never give me the money to pay for this. I can barely get five rupees from him for my own expenses.'

'Well, I will pay for it,' she said with a half smile. Then slipping her right arm around his neck she rested her face against his shoulder.

'Where do you have the money to pay for it?' asked Cornelis, and holding her head in his hands he pressed his cheek against her hair.

'I have my gold jewellery,'

The words that fell from her lips had a lyrical sound. The scent of her hair, dampened with perfumed water, the sweet-smelling powder on her neck, her breath, enchanted Cornelis like a flower-scented breeze. He held her head in his hands and gazed into her face. Her eyes, lowered, brimful of love, shone like blue sapphires. Between her lips, parted in a shy smile, her small, very white, pearl like teeth gleamed.

Cornelis had not thought there could be such sweetness in a wife.

'No', he said firmly, 'we will certainly not sell your gold jewellery.'

-Translated by Ranjini Oboyosokoro

Going Back

When my mother left the school at Yatalamatta where she taught for twenty-six years, the people of the village gave her a big farewell. I had an invitation from the organizing committee. It said the function would be on March 25 and that a group photograph would be taken afterwards. I didn't go. I can't say this was for want of leisure. Some time ago I had taken part in a ceremony of this kind when Mr Wiratunga of the boys' school was leaving. I am still nauseated when I remember the blubbering and the blathering on that occasion. I knew there would be the same sort of exhibition when mother was leaving. I had no stomach for such silliness; village folk who wore their hearts on their sleeves seemed to me clods who were incapable of thinking rationally. Even as I took up the invitation I could imagine Mother trying to make a speech and breaking down; her eyes running with tears and her voice shaken by sobs. 'What a blessing that I can stay here and not be mixed up in such stuff and nonsense,' I said to myself.

It was for this reason that I went home during the holiday only a week before the Sinhalese New Year. When I got home the first thing both Mother and *Nangi* asked me even before I could change my clothes, was why I hadn't come to the function.

'It was very rude of you,' Mother said, 'You shouldn't have stayed away when they sent you a letter all the way to the University.'

'Quite so, if Podi *Aiya* had been there everything would have been just perfect,' *Nangi* joined in.

'Yes, if I'd come I would have cried, too,' I said.

'Of course, you would have been the first to cry, if you'd come,' *Nangi* retorted. 'In spite of all your big talk, I know you'd have cried before anyone else.'

'Don't talk nonsense! These farewells are good for women who are waiting to turn on the tap,' I said angrily. *Nangi's* remark seemed to me an insult to my mature intelligence.

'He got these ideas into his head after he started reading big books,' said *Nangi*. 'But when we were at Ratnasara together, he'd be all excited at the very mention of home. When we'd gone back after the holidays he'd talk of nothing else for two or three days.

'Do you hear, Mother?' she went on. 'He talks like a lord now but when we were children he'd chatter to me all the time about home once you'd left us at school. 'Now Mother must be going back.' 'Now she must be gathering vegetables in the back garden.' 'Now she must be offering flowers at the shrine.' That's all he'd talk about. But now he can't come back to the place where we lived for twenty-six years even on the day we are leaving.'

I hid my blushes.

'It wasn't really because of my exam that I stayed away,' I said in irritation. 'It was because I didn't want to watch that sort of comedy.'

'Never mind the function. You must come with me to Yatalamatta before the New Year. I have nobody to go with. I was waiting for you,' said Mother.

'Why do you want to go back to the village you have left? There is none of your family there,' I said scowling.

'That's not the point. But at least at the New Year we must call on people who were our neighbours for so many years.'

'I can't. I have a lot of work to get through. I've brought down all my books.'

'Well, if you can't, I'll go alone. It wouldn't be very difficult for me to take the jeep that goes to Yatalamatta early in the morning,' Mother said to me reproachful by.

She said no more at the time. But after lunch the next day I heard her talking again to *Nangi* about the journey. I was at the dining table, reading a book and I could hear them talking in the bedroom.

'It's the seventh today—nearly two weeks since we came away—and I still haven't been able to go,' Mother was complaining.

'Much use it was waiting for Podi *Aiya!*' I heard *Nangi* say. 'The only thing to do now is to go by yourself, Mother.'

'I don't know what state the place is in already. When we left I told the school-mistress from Hettihena to open the doors of the school every few days and sweep the front garden at least. It is the season now when the rubber leaves fall and the whole garden must be covered with them.'

'If the Hettihena teacher isn't ill she won't fail to do as you said,' *Nangi* answered her.

'It is all right if she does it. But I am not sure, when I was there things got done because people were afraid. But it won't be the same now. And I couldn't get the gate repaired before I came away. Both posts were rotten. If that wretch of a bull from Pelawatta has got into the garden, he'll have ruined everything. A fine state things must be in!'

I was both amused and provoked by this conversation.

'Why give yourself all this trouble? When you left you should have brought the school here—garden and all. Then you wouldn't have had all this worry. It won't do the Government good to have you always hanging around like a creditor,' I said mockingly.

The two of them went on talking as if they hadn't heard me.

Mother spent the next evening on preparations for the visit to Yatalamatta. She got some sheaves of betel leaves as gifts for several people there.

'But betel leaves alone won't do. I must take a tin of biscuits too, to Rukmalgoda,' she remarked to *Nangi* while putting the betel together.

'And Brampy! You can't sleep late tomorrow. We must take the jeep early in the morning. We'll have to get to Unanvitiya and walk from there,' she added to our servant who was by her.

'Why get off at Unanvitiya?' asked *Nangi*. 'You can go straight to Yatalamatta. '

'How? The Anguruvela bridge is broken down and the jeep now runs on the Unanvitiya road. But it is nothing to walk the three miles from there. We can be at Yatalamatta by ten anyway,' Mother replied enthusiastically.

'If there is any trouble it'll be crossing the *edanda* at Danduvana.' She went on. I hope the water has come up to the *edanda*. Otherwise I'll feel giddy when I see the bottom. Still, I'll get across somehow. Or if I can't, I'll at least get the Kumara girl to help me over by way of Mahahena.'

Mother's voice was so eager that I felt she was already making the journey in her imagination.

'If we have to walk from Unanvitiya we want get to

Yatalamatta before eleven or twelve,' complained Brampy.

'Twelve or two—what does it matter? We are going back to the place which was our home, aren't we?' Mother replied.

That night, before going to bed, *Nangi* came up to me while I was studying.

'If you don't go with Mother tomorrow, she'll get into a lot of trouble,' she said. 'Now she wants to take that fool Brampy. If she goes with him, she will fall off an *edanda* and break her neck. Please go,' *Nangi* pleaded.

'That would serve her right for having the nerve to plan these jaunts,' I said.

'That may be. But please go with her, Podi *Aiya*. Otherwise she will get into some trouble.'

'I don't want to go on this ridiculous journey! I must finish this book before the holidays are over. If I go, tomorrow will be spent on the trip. The day after, I'll have to rest my legs. I shan't be able to do any work.'

'Anyway, please go, Podi *Aiya,'* *Nangi* repeated.

'No, I can't. She can take anybody she has asked. Let her go and learn a lesson.'

In spite of what I said then, I decided, after *Nangi* went away, to accompany Mother after all. If Mother got an idea into her head, she would carry it out, anyhow. I too felt that if she went with Brampy she might get into some mess. So, while still inwardly murmuring against it, I decided reluctantly to go.

Although we left home the next morning before dawn, it was about seven when the jeep arrived. Mother had several parcels in her hand,, but I didn't want to help her with any of them because of the resentment in my heart. We were the only passengers in the jeep; Mother took a seat at the rear, while I sat by the driver.

The gravelled road from Hammeliya to Unanvitiya passed through some pretty country. On one side of the road lay fields of open heath, on the other side, low hills covered with tea bushes, coconut, breadfruit or jak trees. Houses lay almost at the edge of the road, with some of thier gardens marked off by hedges of green stakes or flowering plants. As we passed by in the jeep, my eyes would rest instinctively from time to time on a young girl sweeping her garden. When we approached Yatalamatta the fields that we had so far seen on one side of the road gave place to the Gin Ganga and its pleasant river bank.

The charm of these surroundings softened my ill temper. When the jeep stopped at the Unanvitiya market place, with its row of shops and its suspension bridge, I alighted with some cheerfulness and took one of the parcels that Mother was carrying.

Yet my feeling of pleasure slowly lessened. Post Estate, which was once full of rubber trees, was now a desert without tree or leaf. I hadn't known that the rubber trees had been uprooted because the land was to be planted with tea. I held the parcel over my head and walked on with quick strides. It was now about eleven; the sun beat on us like fire and the sandy road was getting hotter. My body was dripping sweat. Both of us hastened on without exchanging a word. Post Estate stretched about a mile and ended at the village of Yatalamatta. That mile seemed to me like ten.

'It's a mercy it'll be shady from here on,' said Mother when we got to the Danduvana *edanda*.

It had been raining in the hills and, as Mother had hoped, the stream was about half full. I took all the parcels from her and went ahead. In place of the bamboo stem that had once served as a hand rail, there was now a fairly thick trunk of an areca nut tree, so crossing the *edanda* was not very difficult.

As we reached the other side, we met Mr. Kumara. 'It looks as though you've come visiting friends and relatives,' he said.

'Yes—how can we forget them so soon?' said Mother, smiling broadly.

'Yes, yes, of course. You may go anywhere, but this village is your real home. Podi Mahattaya's especially,' he added turning to me. 'You were born here, weren't you?'

'Well, wherever I live is home to me,' I said with deliberate indifference.

'Don't say that. When you are a big man someday and people say you were born here, we'll all be honoured.'

Everybody we ran into thereafter had the same thing to ask, 'Ah, coming back to visit your old home?' 'Of course, how can you forget so soon a place where you lived so long?' Some of our acquaintances turned to me and asked, 'Has Podi Mahattaya just come home for the holidays?' By the bridge we encountered Hichchi Mahattaya who said, 'It was very bad of you not to have come even when we sent you a letter.' He had been on the farewell committee. It seemed to me that all this was foolishness and empty chatter. 'What a pack of sentimental idiots,' I said to myself.

Near the bridge we also met Loku Mahattaya of Pelawatta, 'We were saying only yesterday that you'd be sure to come today or tomorrow — before the New Year anyway,' Loku Mahattaya exclaimed loudly. His property was next to the school.

'Ah well, it's only today I was free to come,' said Mother. 'How are things at the school? I told the school mistress from Hettihena to go every two or three days and see that the place was kept clean. I don't know whether she has done that.'

'I haven't seen her. I couldn't go there myself after you left. Are you going straight to the school or to Rukmalgoda?' he asked. 'But why go to the school? There is nobody there now.'

'We'll go to Rukmalgoda first and have something to eat. Then we must go to the school,' Moher said.

Her eagerness seemed to me to have grown with these encounters and conversations on the way and she had grown more talkative too.

It was almost twelve when we reached Rukmalgoda.

'We knew you'd come today,' said Akmeemana Hamine as soon as she saw us. 'We waited for some time before sitting down to lunch. And when did Podi Mahattaya come home?'

After we had washed our faces, we were taken to the dining table. Even while eating, Mother kept asking Akmeemana Hamine questions about the school.

'Haven't you seen that girl from Hettihena going that way?' she asked.

'How should she be going there? As soon as the holidays began her husband came down and took her off to Hikkaduwa,' answered Akmeemana Hamine.

'Well, well, with all my pleading I haven't been able to make her spend the holidays here!'

'Good Lord, school teachers today don't do anything except for pay! You won't find teachers like yourself now!'

'That foolish generation is gone now!' I answered.

Although by the end of the meal I was so drowsy that I could hardly keep my eyes open mother set out for the school without wasting a moment.

'I've never got mixed up in such an annoying business before.' I grumbled to myself as I accompanied her. The school was about half a mile from Rukmalgoda. Fortunately, the fierce glare of the sun had somewhat lessened now and there was some shade; yet the tarred road seemed as hot under our feet as if it had been on fire.

As we passed the bend in the road near the temple, we caught sight of the school garden and the high walls of the school house. Even from the first glimpse, they had the air of a place that was deserted. Coming closer we could distinguish the fence of Rukattana trees and the gate. The trees with their wildly overgrown branches pushing out above the road, made my first impression stronger. We came up to the gate And I drew aside the bamboo stems which served as bars. In the enveloping stillness, the grating sound of the bamboo seemed to resound loudly. 'No one has even stepped in here since we left!' Mother remarked as we passed through the gate. 'Just look at how the grass has overgrown the garden in a few days!'

The garden was covered not only with grass, but also with dried rubber leaves blown by the wind.

The door of the school house creaked as I opened it. As always during the holidays, desks and benches were piled in the hall. Scattered here too on the floor were leaves and litter carried by the wind.

What I needed most was a short nap. I put two benches together, took off my coat and lay down. 'Wake me when the sun is low,' I told Mother.

Lying there, I looked up at the school roof. It shared the desolation of a place where no one had set foot for some time. Large cobwebs hung here and there and, as I looked, two white-bellied mice ran idly between the rafters. Soon my eyes closed.

When I woke, I realized I must have been asleep for over an hour. I lay where I was and glanced around. Mother was working in the garden with a *mamoty*. 'Cease, cease—' I listened to the rasping sound of the *mamoty* as it struck the hard earth with a monotonous rhythm. On the roof, the two mice I had seen before I fell asleep were still gamboling among the rafters. 'How many cobwebs there are up there!' I thought. I felt sleepy again, as if my tiredness had grown.

'Dear, dear, who would have thought the place would

come to this?' Mother was muttering to herself as she worked.

I turned my head and looked out through the large window. The sun had now set behind the hills which lay beyond the road, and they looked faded and weary after their long scorching.

I rose unwillingly and began to walk up and down the school house to rid myself of the sluggish feeling in my body. Mother was still working in the garden.

'Cease, cease—' the sound of the *mamoty* alone broke the silence.

I strolled about aimlessly for some time, then leant against a parapet and looked on. At the other end of the parapet lay a blackened clay lamp and a basket with withered flowers in it. It occurred to me that Mother must have lit the lamp before she came away.

'What's this lamp?' I asked her.

'Which one? The one on the wall? That's the lamp we lit for the gods before we left.'

I threw the dried-up flowers out of the basket and put it back on the parapet. Then I thought it shouldn't be left lying there and put it inside a cupboard.

The schoolroom felt lonelier than ever and I stepped out into the garden. Tufts of grass had sprouted everywhere, and there were marks left by rainwater which must have flooded the garden some days ago. I sat down on the plinth. Only the orange tree was as I remembered it. I gazed at the big roots which stood up out of the earth. What times we had spent, *Nangi* and I, as children sitting at its foot. Was it really the same tree? I looked at it again. One or two of its branches were dying. Some one had told me that fruit trees did not flourish where no human voice was heard. I got up and went where mother was working.

'Who would have thought this place would come to such a state? It'll take a month to clear. I started working with this *mamoty* because I couldn't bear to see things as they were,' she said to me, as I stood there in silence. 'It must be nearly five now. This part at least looks all right now.'

She took the *mamoty* in and left it inside the school. She seemed tired as she came back and sat down on the front step wiping her face. I sat down by her and both of us were silent for a while.

'How long it is since we first came here! There was only this one schoolroom then.' Mother broke the silence.

'These walls, none of this was here then. None of it would have been put up but for me.' She went on talking, and I listened.

'I got this plinth made when I was expecting your sister—the one who died. I spent three years getting these walls and fences put up, and filling the swamps down there. That piece of flat land was a thicket with bushes up to a man's head. Ah, well, the place is going back to what it was. That wall has been cracked by rain water.'

While she was talking, I felt a pang that could not be put into words. This decay—was it not going on before my eyes, as I contemplated the trees, the schoolroom, the walls? They were shrinking into a desolation which touched my heart.

Mother began to speak again, pausing from time to time.

'You were a child, just beginning to run about, when I finished all this work, built that room and cemented the school floor. The footprints you left in the cement should be there even now. One day, when the cement was still wet, we had gone to Galle. When we got back, we went round to the back door and opened it, and you ran into the schoolroom before I could stop you. The marks you left must be there, clear as ever,' she said, and rising, went up to the door opening from the schoolroom into the headmistress's quarters.

'There, you see—there are your prints,' she said, pointing. 'I shouted, "No, no, son, this way!" Those are the marks you made running back.' She showed me another line of foot prints in the opposite direction. 'They'll remain there till the floor is cemented again.' I was bending over to look at the prints. They made me want to touch them. I bent right down and felt them with my hands. The big toe, the other toes, the heel—they were all there. I turned my head and looked at my feet. A strange happiness passed through me, like falling in love. 'They are mine! Aren't these all mine?' I said to myself. My eyes were wet. Everything around me seemed to dissolve in the flood of tenderness that swept my heart.

'It's time to go. I want to take this lime plant home and grow it. If you can uproot it without hurting the roots we can replant it there,' Mother said, getting up from the step.

'I'll take it out of the ground,' I said. I brought the *mamoty* and uprooted the plant, leaving a clod of earth sticking to the roots. Mother wrapped it in a large leaf and tied it. 'Let's wash our faces and get ready to go.'

I went down to the well with Mother and washed. The water was very cold against my face—refreshingly cold. I dipped my face into the hollow of my hands filled with water and also drank several mouthfuls.

'I must drink some of the water too, before going, however cold it is,' said Mother.

As I put the bamboo back in place on our way out, I felt a sharp pain within me. Something seemed to fall away from my heart—something that would be lost forever. It was now almost twilight.

We walked silently until we passed the boundary of the school garden and more than once I looked back.

'Let me see that lime plant,' said Mother, who had not spoken a word till the school was out of sight. She took the plant from me and examined it.

'A fine plant. It will grow nicely in our front garden.'

I looked back again after we had turned the bend. The high, cream-coloured walls of the school could just be seen through the trees.

We waited at the corner of the road for the jeep for more than half an hour. It was about seven when it arrived at last. There was another young man waiting with us. He was going to Colombo by way of Baddegama; he had a suitcase in his hand, and he wore a pair of white slippers that would have suited a woman better than a man. There was an old woman with him and from their talk I realized that she was his mother and had come to see him off.

'When you get there you must write to us every two or three days,' she kept saying.

The young man made no reply for some time. At last he said angrily, 'What's the use of making the Postal Department richer? Colombo isn't a far off country, as you imagine. Anyway, I shan't have the leisure to write so often.'

His words made me smile. The jeep arrived and we got in—the three of us.

'Such foolish women, these village folk,' the young man remarked to me after the jeep had started. 'They don't give you any peace from the time you leave home.'

The headlights were bad and the jeep moved slowly. There were many ruts in the road, and whenever a wheel went into one of them we were shaken. Each time this happened, the thorns of the lime plant scraped my feet.

Little by little, the jeep filled up with passengers. Among those who got in were several people I knew. Two of them, the registrar from Unanvitiya and the retired police officer, spoke to me.

'How long is it till your final exam?' the registrar asked me in a respectful tone.

'Another year,' I said.

'And then you'll be a doctor. Good for us too,' he remarked.

'So many rich men there have been in these villages, but none of their sons could pass a decent examination.'

'What's this you are taking?' He was pointing at the plant at my feet. 'A lime plant, isn't it? What? Carrying away an ordinary lime plant?'

'Yes, Mother wanted to take it home from Yatalamatta,' I said with assumed nonchalance.

Both my acquaintances got off at the next stop. I moved into a corner of the jeep and reflected. If I had stayed at home, I could have worked at my books the whole day. This journey had been a waste of time. How silly my behaviour had been earlier in the evening! My mind shrank from recollecting it and I was ashamed of myself. How immature I had been!

The jeep jerked us from side to side, and the lime plant kept knocking against my feet. Every time it touched me, I was irritated. I put it in a corner but with the shaking of the jeep it rolled back to my feet.

The jeep stopped for somebody to get out. I took the plant and stealthily threw it far out of the window.

When we reached home, it was about eight-thirty. My head was aching, so I went to my room and stretched myself out on the bed in a bad humour. I could hear Mother at the dining table talking to *Nangi*.

'The whole place is a jungle. Grass grown wild in the garden, the lamp and flowers we left in the schoolroom still there, leaves and dust, and rubbish all over. I could have cried when I saw it. Lord, to think that that was the place I kept so well!'

I tossed in my bed, as if in pain, and cursed. I cursed myself and my miserable education.

But Mother's voice was flowing as if infused with new life.

-Translated by Reggie Siriwardena

SARANA

I first came to know Sarana through George Van der Bona. I'm quite clear in my mind about that. But how I first met Van der Bona or where, I cannot now recall, try as I might. I can only say that I began to bump into him, seemingly by chance, on several occasions, in various different places. At first, I didn't take much notice of him. Quite often he happened to be in the company of someone I knew, so that while talking to my friend I would exchange a polite word or two with him. But in those days I hardly knew who or what he was.

Perhaps it was because he seemed to know so much about me that I first began to take some interest in him. I gathered from his conversation that he was familiar with my stories, written before I joined the Broadcasting Corporation, and that he listened in to my programmes. It was hard to believe that he, a Burgher, would listen to Sinhala programmes.

In time I realized that Van der Bona was very different from the normal run of Burghers. Although he generally spoke in English, I found, in the occasional word or two of Sinhala I heard him use, that there was hardly a trace of an accent. Whenever he met me he would talk of Sinhala books, or plays, or local arts and crafts. How was A's recent play? What do you think of B's new collection of short stories? Why has M not written anything recently? Was C's dance recital a success? These were the questions he invariably asked me, and often finding it difficult to answer them I grew impatient with him. 'He picks up these various morsels from here and there and then displays them for my benefit,' I thought.

But I was amazed at his thorough knowledge of certain subjects. I realized that he knew far more than I did about Kandyan dancing. Perhaps he had acquired this knowledge through his long residence in the Kandyan area. He spoke of the dancer Gunaya or the drummer Ukkuwa as if he had associated with them closely and knew them personally. One day, comparing the dancing of Gunaya with that of Kiri Ganithaya he made such perceptive criticisms that he evoked my secret admiration. Besides I was ashamed by my own ignorance of such subjects.

'What Ranmala is doing is quite wrong, isn't it?' he asked me once quite suddenly. Not knowing what he was talking about I was momentarily taken aback. 'The man is corrupting our Kandyan dance forms,' he continued. 'Is it right that he should degrade our national art for the benefit of some tourists who come to the big hotels?'

It made me smile to hear him, a Burgher, refer to Kandyan dance as 'our national art' but I realized almost immediately that I was wrong to laugh at him. If Burghers who had lived in Ceylon for several generations wanted to stake a claim to our cultural heritage what was wrong with that? It was rare enough to find, even in a Sinhalese, that kind of concern or involvement.

'No, it's not right that they should adulterate tradition. Tourists should be shown indigenous art,' I said on that occasion, trying not to display my ignorance.

'Why don't you write radio plays now, Premaratne? I haven't heard one in a long while.' To this question, frequently asked by Van der Bona, I invariably replied that I had no time for creative writing. It was nearly three years now since I had joined the Broadcasting Corporation. It was true that prior to this I had written plays and directed programmes. In fact, I got the job because of my experience in radio work. I joined the Corporation in the hope that I would find more opportunities for such activities. But what happened was completely the opposite. From nine in the morning till noon I sat in my office attending to letters and other administrative chores such as drawing up programme schedules. In the afternoons till five or six I was engaged in the work of the studios.

One day, Van der Bona made a suggestion. 'Come to Galaha for a holiday,' he said. 'It is quiet there and much cooler than Colombo. I will see to all your needs. You are entitled to over a month's vacation every year. So why not make use of it?'

It struck me then that I had not taken any leave since I joined Radio Ceylon. I had not taken leave because I had not known what to do with it. I had often thought of going somewhere on a vacation with my wife and child. But since the expenditure for such a project was considerable I kept postponing it.

This was the first time that an invitation such as Van der Bona's had come my way. How good it would be if we could all three go there. I thought to myself. But Van der Bona was a bachelor and I realized that it would not be fair to descend on him with my family. Besides I did not know him too well. He had invited me, and that too in order to offer me a chance to write. If I accepted his invitation I felt I should go alone.

I told my wife, Sumana, of Van der Bona's invitation. 'Go, Prema, you need a holiday. You work too hard. Everybody keeps telling me that you are growing thin,' she said.

'I wasn't thinking of going there for just a vacation. I must write something. Ever since I accepted this damned job I've had no time for writing.'

'Yes, that's true. If you go on like this you may soon forget how to write. Even my friends ask me why your plays no longer come over the air. They liked your earlier work very much.'

'I'd prefer it if all three of us could go.'

My conscience pricked me that I had not taken my wife on a vacation for so many years. Her work as a school teacher and the work of the household taxed her considerably and I realized that a holiday was essential for her too. It struck me then that she had grown considerably thinner. 'We can all go together some other time. We'll have to wait for the school holidays for that. You go on this trip since you've already had an invitation. Come back with at least one play written,' she said cheerfully.

Her words gave me some relief. I was able to tell myself that I was going not on a vacation but to do some work. I had already worked out the basic plots for several plays. I knew of course that after so long it would not be easy to get down to the actual job of writing. But if I could at least make a start, then I felt I could come back home and continue with it.

Van der Bona was the superintendent of a tea estate named Dalcombe Estate situated about five miles from Galaha. I got off at Peradeniya railway station and took a taxi to the estate. It was about seven-thirty in the evening when I arrived there.

He was waiting at home for me.

'Why did you waste money on a taxi?' If you had told me you were coming up by train I would have met you at the station,' he said. Since I was already going to be the recipient of his hospitality I had not wanted to bother him further and so had merely mentioned that I was coming to Galaha that evening, without giving details.

Van der Bona's house, like that of all tea estate superintendents, was equipped with every comfort. It suddenly struck me that he was probably able to keep it so well because he did not have any children to mess it up. But then he did not have a wife either. All the work of the household was probably done by a man-servant. Or was it a maid? I thought it might be a maid because everything in the household seemed to suggest a feminine touch. Men servants were lazy and knew nothing of order and cleanliness. But I found it hard to believe that Van der Bona being a bachelor would keep a maid as his household help. Perhaps his man-servant was as good as a woman at household tasks. I recalled the servant boy in our household. He, of course, knew nothing of cleanliness or order.

My curiosity to see Van der Bona's servant was soon satisfied. We chatted for a while in the living room, then he took me inside. 'I've got a room ready for you, Prema. You can write at leisure here,' he said.

The room he had set apart for me immediately appealed to me. It was as if he had planned it to create the environment needed for writing. On one side was a beautiful writing desk. Van der Bona pressed a switch and the light on the writing table came on. The way in which it illuminated one part of the table and cast a modulated glow on the rest of the room caught my imagination and I felt I could very easily sit down there and write with concentration.

'Here's a writing table for you. When you look out of

the window during the day you can see the distant hills. It's a beautiful view.' Beside the table was a small bookcase. I was particularly pleased to see there a volume of the complete works of Maupassant. Although I had read a number of Maupassant's short stories I had never had the opportunity to read his longer works which many people praised. Even if I do nothing else I can at least enjoy my vacation reading those stories, I thought to myself.

The bed at the other side of the room was equally pleasing. Looking at it I felt the comforting sensation of warmth that the cool climate of Galaha called for. On a small cupboard by the bed-head was yet another electric light. How pleasant it would be to lie in bed and read till I fell asleep, I thought. I liked to read in bed. At home, too, I was used to doing so. But since I did not have a bedside light my eyes soon ached.

Suddenly, a man in a sarong and a long-sleeved white shirt appeared and stood silently by the door.

'Sarana, you know this gentleman don't you?' Van der Bona asked him. 'You hear him often on the radio. You must have listened to some of his plays. This gentleman has come here to write some plays. If he writes a good one it will be a great honour to us, too. We can listen to it on the radio, and tell ourselves that it was written here. You must look after this gentleman well. Bring him a cup of tea when he gets up in the morning. At other times inquire if he needs any tea or orange juice and see that he gets it. Did you put a clean towel out in the bath room?'

'I was about to do so sir,' said Sarana in a shrinking tone. 'What time would you like dinner?'

'There's no hurry yet. Are you hungry?' Van der Bona asked me.

'No, let's eat later. I had a sandwich on the train around five.'

As Van der Bona was introducing me I observed his servant. I could not understand why my friend described me in such glowing terms to him. I doubted whether Sarana ever listened to the radio, let alone to my plays. I did not see even a flicker of interest on his face at the mention of those things. Sarana appeared to me to be a foolish stolid-looking peasant. He had the broad jaw bones, prominent cheek bones and square face common to many people in the hill country. It was difficult to tell his age. His teeth were discoloured and slightly protruding. But this could be the result not of age but of constant betel-chewing. His hair which was combed back and tied in a small knot had no more than two or three grey strands. A few wrinkles on his face and some prominent veins on his hands gave him a rather mature appearance. I decided, however, that he could not be more than thirty-five years old.

I had washed, changed and had been lying down on the bed for a while when I heard Van der Bona call me. He was seated in the living room. On a small table were two bottles of beer and a bottle of gin. There were also a couple of bottles of what looked like tonic water.

'Shall we have a drink Prema? You must be tired,' he said. 'Yes I'll have some beer. I'm very thirsty,' I said.

While we were drinking, Sarana appeared once or twice bringing in some dishes of fried *haal messa* and some sliced radish. I had never eaten radish as an hors-d'oeuvre so I asked Van der Bona what it was when he held out the plate to me.

'It's one of Sarana's ideas. It is radish. I don't know where he learned it. But it is very good with drinks.'

We sat talking till late into the night. Van der Bona, though he was a planter, did not spend his time at the club playing billiards or poker like the rest of his friends. He could make intelligent conversation whether it was politics, economics or space research. I saw that he had read almost all the important literature published recently in English. I, who should have been better read than him on this subject, was familiar only with the reviews that had appeared in journals.

However, hearing him talk of Sinhala literature and Ceylonese arts and crafts I often wondered whether there was not something false or phoney about his interest. Such doubts arose in me perhaps because of my tenacious belief that a Burgher like him could not possibly feel a sincere attraction towards things Ceylonese. I told myself that it was time I discarded my doubts. In spite of my efforts, however, these inner doubts seemed to strengthen rather than diminish. I could never figure out whether the opinions he expressed about a subject like Kandyan dancing, were those he had picked up from someone else and merely repeated, or whether they sprang from his own inner convictions. I wondered whether what Van der Bona was trying to do, was to assert that though he was a Burgher he was also a Ceylonese and that though he could not consider himself heir to the total heritage of Mother Lanka he could at least claim some part of it. In short he was asking not to be treated as a foreigner but to be given a place in this island. If so, I told myself, I should feel a sense of sympathy and respect towards him rather than attempt to decry his efforts.

'Shall we eat?' he asked and I glanced at the time. I was surprised to find that it was ten minutes to twelve. How quickly time had passed! 'Yes, let's eat. It is already very late,' I said. Van der Bona then called out 'Sarana! Dinner!'

Immediately, Sarana, carrying a dish of rice in one hand and a dish of curry in the other, appeared from nowhere like the genie of Aladdin's lamp. Where had he been all this while? Had he just sat around till so late in the night with the dinner all prepared waiting for his master's summons? Or had he been asleep? How, then, could he have appeared so promptly carrying two dishes in his hands? He made several trips to and from the kitchen, and the manner in which he miraculously brought forth various dishes and placed them on the table was truly amazing. The food was steaming hot as if it had just come off the fire. How had he kept the food hot and yet waited so long for us?

He had prepared a dish of yellow rice for the main course. I do not know whether it was my tiredness, or the cool climate, or the beer I had drunk, but that rice seemed so flavourful to me, that it sent waves of pleasure coursing through my veins.

'Your cook is excellent,' I said admiringly. Van der Bona's face lit up. 'I call this "Sarana's Special"!' he said. 'Whenever an important guest arrives he produces this dish. I don't have to tell him.' Sarana was standing silently by. His face showed no sign of response to my praise. For some time we ate silently.

'Are you not dancing in a *Suvisi Vivarana* ceremony in the next few days?' Van der Bona asked Sarana suddenly. Realizing that I was taken aback by the question, Van der Bona smiled. In fact I had turned to look at Sarana in some surprise. His face had a look I had not seen before. What had seemed faded and stolid was suddenly alight with new life. His sunken eye-balls seemed straining to jumps out of their sockets. 'Yes, there is one next *Poya* day. Not the *Poya* that falls in a day or two but the following full moon night.' At every word his body seemed to quiver with excitement.

'A pity; isn't there one earlier than that?' We must take this gentleman to see you perform,' Van der Bona said glancing at me.

'Is Sarana a dancer?,

'Sarana is a very famous dancer. There is not a village in this neighbourhood which will perform a *Suvisi Vivarana* ceremony without him.' He replied.

'Very good. I have never seen that ceremony performed. We don't have them in our area. I would very much like to see Sarana dance. Next time, I'll come up specially to see a performance.'

I awoke the next morning with a sense of tremendous well-being in body and mind. I opened my eyes and spent a long time just lying in bed listening. Apart from the distant barking of a dog and the cawing of a crow there was no sound. I got out of bed and looked at the time. It was twenty past eight. Just then Sarana entered with a cup of tea. The only sounds he could have heard from my room were the rustle as I stepped out of bed and the light shuffle of my slippered feet.

'Is your master awake.' I asked him.

'Yes, he went to work a long time ago,' he said with a slight smile. 'He leaves by seven-thirty every day. 'It was then that I remembered that work on plantations began at down.

I had just completed my morning wash and finished dressing when Sarana arrived again in my room to say that breakfast was ready.

I finished breakfast, sat at my table and began to write. I started working on a theme I had long had in mind for a radio play. About ten-thirty I began to feel quite thirsty. It would be good if I could have drink. At that very moment Sarana appeared with a glass of grapefruit. It struck me how fortunate my friend was to obtain the services of a man like Sarana. He seemed born for domestic service. He could sense instinctively his master's needs. It was unnecessary to order him. Even before one could make a request, Sarana had anticipated it and complied with it. He seemed to me a man who did not have any private life or individuality apart from his role of domestic servant. His mind seemed totally conditioned to servitude and born of servitude. If he conceived an affection or loyalty to a person, he seemed like the type who would soon allow himself to be transformed into a mere shadow of that person. I could not understand how such a person could also be an artist. After all, hard work never produced an artist. An artist must necessarily have some kind of individuality. I even began to have doubts about the truth of Van der Bona's statements about Sarana. When he arrived with the glass of juice, therefore, I was tempted to question him about his private life.

Even after half an hour's conversation what I learned about him was infinitesimal. I rarely got a direct answer to a question. He gave me to understand that he was only one of the less important dancers at the *Suvisi Vivarana* ceremony and at the village temple. Van der Bona had made him out to be one of the best dancers in the entire region. If so, why had he not confined himself to his profession as a dancer instead of taking to domestic service? 'Is it difficult for you, Sarana, to make a living out of dancing? Are you forced to take on other jobs?' I asked him frankly. He smiled foolishly at me as if he totally missed the seriousness of my question.

'One or two people hold land from the Tooth temple. They just perform once a year at the annual *perahera* at Kandy. They've enjoyed those lands for generations.'

'Do you often get invited for performances?' 'No, very rarely. Now not even as much as formerly. For the last three or four months there have been no ceremonies.'

I realized then that the facts about Sarana were in reality quite different to what my friend had made them out to be. It was almost as if it was a matter of great pride for him to claim to have a famous Kandyan dancer as his domestic servant. Did he speak in that way without any real knowledge of Sarana's position? Or had he just not bothered to find out the true facts about Sarana's life? Was it merely that he obtained a vicarious pleasure playing the role of a feudal chieftain in claiming that he had a skilled dancer as part of his domestic retinue?

About six months later, I happened to meet Van der Bona again in Colombo. 'Come with me to Galaha,' he suggested. 'It is time to write a new play. The other one was very good. Sarana still talks about it.'

On the last occasion I had written two plays, one complete, the other in outline. When I knew it was going to be broadcast I had written to Van der Bona asking him to listen in. He had done so and had later written to me praising it.

I realized that unless I went away to some place like that to write, I would never get any useful work done. Sumana, who also liked what I had written the last time, agreed with me heartily.

'Go away for three or four days once in a while and write something. Then you'll get some satisfaction. Otherwise you'll soon tire of this job.'

I hesitated to make a convenience of Van der Bona's hospitality but I felt that his invitation to me was sincere. It was also convenient to go up in his car. I therefore took three days' leave which together with the weekend gave me a five-day break and set off with Van der Bona.

It was on that occasion that I learned that Sarana had become a film fan. One night he did not come to serve at dinner. Seeing Van der Bona himself go into the kitchen to serve out the meal I went to help him.

'Don't bother, Prema. The man cooks everything, puts the dishes out, lays the table before he leaves. I have only to dish out the food,' he said as I walked into the kitchen.

'Where is he? Has he gone home for a dance ceremony?'

'No. He has gone to the cinema.'

'Does Sarana go to films?' I asked in surprise.

Van der Bona laughed. 'He is mad about films now. He sees every single new film that comes out. What is more, he reads all the film magazines. Come this way a minute.'

He took me to the back of the house. In front of the kitchen adjoining the pantry was a small room.

'This is his room,' said Van der Bona opening the door and walking in.

On the jute bed on which Sarana slept, I saw several magazines with pictures of actresses on their covers. Furthermore, the walls were covered with pin-ups of film stars cut from magazines and newspapers. I laughed when I saw them.

'Well, well, our Kandyan dancer has now become a film addict. It's hard to believe,' I said.

'It doesn't matter after all. The man is an artist himself. Now that he doesn't get much of a chance to dance I thought it would be good for him to get some satisfaction from this sort of thing. He goes at least twice a week. He never misses a new film.'

'How did he first get involved with this?'

'I once went to Weerabaddana's film *Maya*. It was the first Sinhala film I had seen. It was very good, wasn't it? So I thought I would send Sarana to see it the next day. That was when he first acquired a taste for films. However, he doesn't care for all types of films. You should hear him come home and criticize them.'

That night at dinner Van der Bona spoke only of Sinhala films. Just as he knew novelists and playwrights, he knew a lot about directors, producers, film actors and actresses. I was sure he must have acquired this information in conversations with Sarana. I did not ask him whether he had seen any other Sinhala films since *Maya*. But I was surprised and could not understand why he should take pride in displaying detailed knowledge of the trashy films that had mushroomed overnight and nobody thought much of. As for me I not only knew nothing about them, but felt it a waste of time to even discuss them. I concluded that Van der Bona talked of films in the same way in which he discussed other important subjects, perhaps because he knew so little about them.

One day when Van der Bona was in his office, Sarana came into my room. He did not come to bring me the usual food or drink, so I looked at him curiously. He had a cutting from a magazine in his hand.

'Sir, they say here that they want Kandyan dancers for a film. Just look at this sir,' he said handing me the cutting. It contained an advertisement to that effect. I took some time to figure out what it was he wanted.

'Well, what about it?' I asked.

'I was thinking of sending an application. We have little chance of betterment unless we get something like that. What future is there for us hanging around here in the backwoods dancing the *Suvisi Vivarana* or an occasional *Kankariya?* If you would put in a word for me, sir, I think I could get the job.'

I thought for a moment, unsure of what to say. 'I don't know any of these film people. Didn't you ask Mr Van der Bona about it'?

'Please, sir, don't mention the matter to him. He won't like it at all because it would mean giving up my job here. It's true he cannot manage without me, but then, how can I stay like this forever?'

'I don't think Mr. Van der Bona will stand in the way of your progress, Sarana.'

'It's not much use telling him anyway. There's little he can do. Only you can help me in this matter. Since you work on the radio you must meet artists and film people.'

'Well, I'll see if I can get in touch with someone in the company which put in the advertisement. But I won't promise anything. These are things one cannot do in a hurry. In any case, send in your application. If you don't get it this time round you might still have a chance on another occasion,' I said, hoping for a little breathing space.

When Sarana left I couldn't help laughing. It struck me afterwards that this might not be just a matter for amusement. If he were to get a false sense of his own talent it might lead not to his betterment but to disaster. But how could I tell him that? If, as Van der Bona claimed, he was in fact a skilled dancer, then may be he could render better service to society in other ways than by spending a life-time in domestic service? I could not make up my mind one way or the other, since I had not seen him dance.

In spite of what Sarana said, I felt I should speak to Van der Bona about him. If Van der Bona was the cause of Sarana's misplaced ambitions then it was his duty to reveal the truth to his servant. Besides, I could then impress on Van der Bona the dangerous effects of such ideas on Sarana's future life.

'What is this transformation that has come over Sarana?' I asked him that evening.

'What transformation?' he asked, as if not expecting my question. I described the incident of Sarana showing me the advertisement and his subsequent request to me. Van der Bona laughed.

'Take no notice of those things. The man has got a touch of 'film madness,' that's all.'

'But if, as you say, he is a good dancer it is worthwhile finding him some such opening. I may not be able to obtain an acting role in films for him, but I have a programme on the radio called 'Unknown Artists'. I could present him one day on that programme. That might give him something of an opening.'

'There's no harm in that. You can interview him on

the radio. It would be a great honour for me, too,' he said laughing.

'But I must know first whether he is in fact a good dancer. The people I have interviewed up to now on that programme have been first rate, even though they were tucked away in distant corners. It would be best if we could see him dance. But then, you are a man who knows a lot about this subject. I could take your word for it.'

'I've never seen the fellow dance myself. Do you think I would waste my time staying up nights to see his *Suvisi Vivarana* and *Kankari* ceremonies?'

For a moment I was speechless. All my doubts about Van der Bona arose again. It was clear to me now, how his mind worked. All he wanted was to create the appearance of being a great lover of Sinhala art. I realized that all his information about Kandyan dancers must have been picked up from others. His knowledge of literature and drama too could hardly be any different. I even began to doubt the sincerity of the motives that prompted him to invite me to his home.

'If you don't know anything about his skill, then I'm certainly not prepared to present him on my programme. I should have to see him dance, otherwise I would have to lie. Besides, the man might get more false ideas about himself then.'

'Don't take this matter so seriously, Prema,' he said, patting me on the back as if admonishing a child (he was in fact ten or twelve years older than me). 'This chap's crazy ideas will vanish after a while. They probably occur to him when he sees you. Forget it all and write another radio play like the last one.'

Although Van der Bona glossed over the matter, doubts continued to lurk in my mind. His speech and actions so far as they related to Sarana seemed to me totally lacking in responsibility.

My next visit to Van der Bona's house was not in order to write but just to enjoy a vacation. I had spent two weeks in hospital for an operation. Van der Bona had heard of my illness on one of his visits to Colombo and came to see me in hospital. I felt that I might have misjudged him. Whatever his original motives may have been for inviting me, I realised on that occasion that his affection for me was sincere. I blamed myself strongly for having entertained the idea that his invitation to me had been merely to satisfy some false pride.

He not only came to see me but invited me to come up to Galaha for a few weeks' convalescence once I left hospital. The doctors, too, advised me to take at least a weeks rest in a pleasant climate. I accepted his invitation.

I remembered, on my way there, the request Sarana had made to me on my previous visit. Perhaps he had forgotten it by now. But what should I tell him if he did happen to ask me? I decided to free myself of all responsibility by telling him frankly that I had no power whatever to do anything for him in this matter.

However, Sarana made no mention of it. It was as if, in the past months, the matter had been totally obliterated. Come to think of it, it was nearly a year now since that last visit. Although we in the cities find that time passes quickly, for one living in this environment the whole incident must seem to have occurred a very long time ago.

I learned, however, of another reason for his loss of interest in the matter. This was something totally unexpected. Sarana was to be married shortly.

Van der Bona told me this news as if it were some marvellously mysterious event. It was as if he were describing the love affair or secret liaison of a famous poet or musician.

'Love has entered the life of our artist,' he began with a smile on his face. I looked at him with interest, anxious to hear more details.

'He has found a girl,' he said.
'Really?'
'Yes, yes, he plans to get married soon.'

I thought that a marriage had been arranged with a girl from his village. One who had a small piece of land and perhaps a house. If so, it would be a good thing for Sarana, I thought. I asked Van der Bona about it.

'Are you joking? It's not anything like that. This is not the traditional arranged affair. It is a case of love at first sight. She's not a village woman. In fact she is a very attractive creature; she must be from Colombo. You should see the way she dresses!' Van der Bona said boastfully.

At the dinner table I glanced several times quite observantly at Sarana. He had an innocent foolish look about him. His humble manner was apparent in every gesture. It was a mystery to me how a beautiful woman, as Van der Bona claimed she was, one who had grown up in a city environment, could possibly be attracted to a man like him. Whatever his mental deficiencies, if he had even the physical attractiveness to ensnare a woman I might not have been surprised. But he didn't.

However, who can tell the intricacies of a woman's mind? A woman falls in love with a man for reasons far different to what we imagine. What different types of men have proved attractive to women? Don't the blind and the lame, too, win women's hearts? Is there not a story in the *Jatakas* about a woman who left her strong sturdy husband to go with a legless cripple? Debating thus, I reassured myself. But I still had a burning curiosity to see Sarana's fiancée. At first, I was reluctant to press Van der Bona for further information, thinking that I might give the impression of being unduly interested in other people's private affairs. I therefore worked round to the subject.

'Where does Sarana's fiancée live? Is she around here?' I asked.

'Yes. If you like I'll show her to you,' he replied at once. 'She lives in Veluppillai's house—the tea-maker. His house is just below there. It's not two months since she came as a domestic servant there.'

In the evening we walked past Veluppillai's house. But nobody was to be seen. After about half-an-hour's walk, we returned again on the same road. Just then a woman carrying a two-year-old child on her hip appeared at the gate. I was immediately reminded of the cover girls on newspapers such as the *Sandarasa*, or the *Alokaya*, but whether it was because of her clothes or the manner in which she had made up her face or how she did her hair I could not definitely say. She was dressed in a grey blouse with a beautifully contrasted red saree. Although her figure was not too attractive (in fact her hips were large and her stomach slightly flabby) she seemed to me to have sufficient feminine charm to make up for these slight inadequacies. She turned her head and the look she flung at me from the corner of her eye made my heart quiver. I stared at her unblinking for several seconds.

As we passed her I glanced at Van der Bona. He had bent his head and was staring at the ground as he walked. 'There she is,' whispered Van der Bona. 'Is *she* Sarana's girl?' I asked amazed.

'Yes, yes, she's the one. What do you think of her? His taste is not too bad, eh? Though he looks such an uneducated peasant his taste is quite that of an artist.'

I did not reply. I could hardly believe that Van der Bona could have been so naive. That an intelligent well-informed man like him should speak so astounded me. For my part, I was moved by a strong sense of concern for Sarana, and a sense of fear for his future. How could he marry a woman like that and continue to live in his village? Though a domestic servant, it was clear that she had the tastes and values of a city girl fed on film fare.

How would she suit a man like Sarana? How could she do the work of a wife in a village household?

That was if you looked at it from Sarana's point of view. From her angle, too, I wondered why she should marry a man like Sarana. Considering her good looks she should not find it too difficult to find a husband from among the young men of the city.

I felt it would not be wrong to question Sarana frankly about this matter. It was too late to stop him now. But perhaps it would not be useless to bring certain problems to his notice even at this stage. I congratulated him on his engagement to begin the conversation. 'Well Sarana, it's a good thing you've decided to marry and settle down,' I said. He looked down shyly and said nothing.

'Do you plan to live in your village once you are married?'

'No, there's no way of living in the village. I must have a job.'

'How will you manage? It will be difficult to continue here in this job?'

'We plan to stay this way for a short time. She's to continue working there, I to stay here. She is acquainted with a film director. He has asked her to come for a part in one of his films. So I also hope to get some kind of an acting role in it. I'm told they plan to introduce some Kandyan dancers in it. I showed you sir, an advertisement some time ago . . .'

'Is it the same director who put in that earlier advertisement? It's a very long time now since it appeared.'

'No, this is someone else. Just wait a minute, I'll show you something,' he said and ran towards the kitchen. I waited, amazed. Sarana quickly returned with a magazine which specialized in gossip about film-stars and showed me a photograph in it. I recognized the face of the girl he was going to marry.

'After the director had seen this picture he made inquiries about Nandawathie. She will be called up very soon. They are starting a new film. Then we plan to go to Colombo and settle down there.'

Should I at this point give Sarana any advice? Was it not my duty to do so? Whether he accepted it or not, should I not honestly tell him that such a marriage was unlikely to bring him happiness? But Sarana's next words totally absolved me of any such responsibility.

'Sir, don't tell the master just yet, but our marriage has already been registered—two weeks ago.'

His face had an expression of sheer happiness. I expressed my congratulations and promised not to tell Van der Bona.

I decided then to forget Sarana's affairs and enjoy my vacation. I slept as late as I pleased and when I woke I lay in bed; read, fell asleep again, and spent my days lazily. Apart from taking an hour's walk in the morning and a half hour's walk in the evenings I did not step out of the house. Van der Bona, too, left me on my own. If I was asleep, he ate alone. On several days we would see each other only at dinner. Sarana was not to be seen around much either. Van der Bona informed me one such evening that Sarana's fiancée had been taken ill and that Sarana had gone to see her in hospital and would be late getting back.

I had decided to take the train down from Kandy on the morning of the *Poya* day. On that day, instead of lazing around in bed as usual, I arose early and began packing my clothes. I went down for breakfast with Van der Bona. I cannot remember whether Sarana was there at the time. Quite often he would put the tea things on the table and leave.

After breakfast, Van der Bona picked up some papers and went into his room. I sat down in the living room and began reading the newspaper. At about eleven I heard a strange sound from the direction of the garage. At first I thought it was the cry of a bull. There must be one around nearby, I thought, and continued to read my paper. I had heard bulls that were being led for slaughter or for branding bellow like that.

Although the sound seemed at first to be far off it began to draw slowly nearer. Once or twice I put down the paper and listened. The sound was becoming more and more frightening. I got up from my chair and was about to call Van der Bona when he came out of his room. His face had a look of terror. His room was close to the garage, so the sound emanating from it must have been very distinct.

'What is that noise?' he whispered.

'Yes, I was wondering what it was myself.' His appearance upset me, too.

'It's coming from the garage. Let's find out,' he said, walking in that direction. 'Where is Sarana? Sarana!' he called, going towards the garage.

On the cold cement floor of the garage, beside the car, Sarana lay sprawled. He breathed with great difficulty. Each time he breathed, that terrible sound we had heard came from his partially-open lips. He was foaming at the sides of his mouth.

I touched him. His body was cold and on shaking it I found it stiff. By his head was a half-empty bottle of insecticide.

'We must rush him to the hospital,' I said.

Van der Bona stared dumbly as if not knowing what to do. There was a look of sheer terror on his face. 'Must we take him to the hospital? Can't we get the apothecary on the estate to see him first?'

'The apothecary will say the same thing. There's nothing we can do by standing around here. His body is almost lifeless already.'

'Then let's inform the police. How do we know what the man has done?'

'If you wait to do all that he will die. Quick, put on a shirt. Lets take him to Kandy. They will inform the police there at the hospital.' Van der Bona was still standing staring blankly, so I took him by the hand and pushed him into the house.

'Hurry, hurry,' I said and went into the house to change into a shirt and a pair of trousers.

Lifting Sarana into the car was not an easy task. We could not put him on to the seat in the sitting position. His body was completely inert. 'Shall I get someone to help?' I asked.

Van der Bona flared at me. 'We don't want anybody. If the neighbours hear of this, what a disgrace it will be,' he said and using all his strength he lifted Sarana, ordered me to sit behind, folded the front seat and put Sarana's feet on it, put his head on my lap and in this manner got him in lengthwise into the car.

Van der Bona drove in silence. One phrase, however, kept forming on his lips. 'I don't know what this goat has gone and done to himself.'

His earlier fears now appeared to have turned into anger. The incident had shattered the order, the quiet of his daily routine, and this I thought was probably the cause of his impatience.

'Has anything happened to that girl? Didn't he say she had been taken to hospital?' But Van der Bona drove on without replying as if he had not heard my question.

Fortunately, the officer in charge of the Out Patient's Department happened to be a friend of Van der Bona's. He immediately ordered that Sarana be taken to the emergency unit and mentioned something about 'Stomach wash.' It was not considered necessary to inform the police.

We stayed about an hour. Later, we learned that the patient had regained consciousness and that he was out of danger. When Van der Bona suggested we return, I asked whether we should inquire about Sarana's girlfriend—in fact his wife.

'I don't want to get mixed up in any of that. What a disgrace it is,' he replied.

'But don't you think we should find out why this man drank insecticide?'

'Who knows whether the girl has deserted him.'

I wanted to say that she was his wife but kept silent because of my promise to Sarana.

'Didn't he say she had been taken to the hospital, sick?'

'We don't know about that either—whether she has gone back or is still there. Why should we go into those matters?'

'Then let's ask Veluppillai. If you don't wish to, I will go and ask him.'

'Don't. Don't. It's not necessary. Let them look after their own affairs. If you wish, I will find out if the girl is still at Veluppillai's. I'll ask the gardener and he will get the information for me.'

It was about three in the afternoon by the time we got back home. I decided to postpone my trip to Colombo by a day or two. 'What will we eat for lunch now? What a nuisance! The things this idiot does! I shall sack him. I will find another servant,' said Van der Bona angrily.

I wondered how Van der Bona would manage without Sarana. It was clear that he was already beginning to feel his absence.

'We can eat whatever there is. Some bread or something. Why bother about food.' I said to soothe him. But I know that Van der Bona would want everything to be as usual. When there was the slightest inadequacy in the meal he would frown. If the meat was a little tough he would scold Sarana or get up and leave the table.

We found when we looked in the kitchen, however, that Sarana had cooked curry and rice for lunch. Since there was also in addition a piece of roast beef, Van der Bona admitted that there would be no problem about dinner either.

Sarana had obviously taken his decision to commit suicide after having planned and organized everything in advance. There must then have been some serious cause for his anguish; I was very curious to find out what it was.

'The girl is no longer at Veluppillai's,' said Van der Bona that same evening.

'I wonder whether she is still in hospital?'

'I don't know. I can't understand what they are doing. I shall be unpopular with my neighbours in future because of this man.'

The next day when Van der Bona went to his office I took a bus to the hospital. I had a gnawing doubt within me that Veluppillai's maid servant might have died. If not, why should Sarana be driven to commit such a terrible act? It wouldn't be surprising if a man like Sarana could not bear that kind of tragedy.

I realised that to get any information about this girl I would have to enlist the help of someone I knew. However, I did not see a single familiar face around. Even the admitting officer was a different man to the one who had been there the previous day. After looking around for about half an hour I finally went up to the 'Inquiries counter. The young man seated at the counter replied to inquiries without so much as turning his head. As a result, nobody understood a word he said. Visitors who inquired about patients and the wards they were in, were totally confused by his answers and stood about, not knowing how to proceed. Realizing that it was little use talking to him, I walked around the counter and entered the office. I went up to a girl seated at a desk who looked like a nurse.

'Forgive me for troubling you,' I said with extreme

politeness. 'I need some information about a patient. It's not about an illness . . . it's some personal information.' I spoke the last sentence with an air of importance. The nurse looked me over curiously. 'Are you from the C.I.D.?' she asked.

It was an unexpected question but I decided to turn it to my advantage. 'I have to conduct an inquiry into a small matter. You don't have to tell too many people,' I whispered in her ear. She became interested immediately. She addressed the young man at the 'Inquiries' counter.

'Take this gentleman and look up the Admission register. Help him to find the information he wants.'

The youth took me to the Registrar's office. 'What is the patient's name?'

'Nandawathie' I said, remembering one of the two names inscribed beneath the photograph Sarana had shown me.

'How can we find someone if you just say the name is Nandawathie?' said the young man smiling contemptuously at me. 'Don't you know the full name?'

'No, I don't know the full name.'

'Well then, do you know the date on which the patient entered?'

'As a matter of face I don't even know that. It was after the thirteenth. Just check the lists for a few days after the thirteenth.'

'How do you expect us to do that? There are four to five hundred names daily entered in this register. If you don't even know the day the patient entered how is one to find this information?' The youth had begun to speak again in the manner he adopted at the inquiry desk. I assumed an authoritative tone. 'I came here for an inquiry, understand. It is because we do not have the information that we are trying to find out these facts. If you cannot do this job go and inform the lady at the desk.' He seemed somewhat subdued by my tone. I saw him silently examine the register and laughed to myself at the role I had assumed.

'There are several Nandawathies,' he said. 'It couldn't be someone who entered the maternity ward could it?'

'No, it couldn't be . . . still, see whether there is anyone by that name there.'

'There is a Nandawathie of Batalawatte who entered the maternity ward on the twelfth.'

'Is she still here? Could I go and check on her? I will have to check on all those by the name of Nandawathie who entered during the last few days. There is no other way to find out the information I want.'

'Well, the person referred to here has had her baby and left two days ago.'

Then it couldn't be the woman I'm looking for, I thought. However, as I could get no further clues I decided to inquire further into that case.

'What is her address? If she came for a confinement she must have given the husband's name.'

The young man smiled his normal contemptuous smile. 'Who knows what names they give for their husbands? When we ask them they just come out with whatever comes to their minds first.'

'See what name is entered there.'

'The husband's name as given here is Sarana. The address is Dalcombe Estate, Galaha.'

I could barely conceal my amazement.

'Then it cannot be the person I want. Sorry for troubling you. I'll come back once I get more information on her case,' I said and left the hospital hurriedly.

I walked around the bookshops in Kandy, had some lunch and returned to Galaha around five in the evening. Van der Bona had come back from the office and was reading the papers in the living room.

'There, he has come' he said to me.

'Who?'

'That fellow Sarana. They've discharged him from hospital. The fool! If he wanted to commit suicide he could have gone home to his village and done it. He didn't have to do it here.'

'Is he well now?'

'I didn't ask him. He doesn't appear to have anything the matter with him now.'

The daily routine at Van der Bona's was resumed. There was no sign that anything untoward had happened. Although I had a strong desire to clarify the whole episode with Sarana, Van der Bona suggested that I should not talk to him about it, so I did not. I did not tell Van der Bona the information I had obtained at the hospital.

'The girl must have gone off with someone else. That's probably why he tried to kill himself. It's a good thing if he forgets all this nonsense, even at this stage, and settles down to his job here,' said Van der Bona.

From then on I did not see Van der Bona for a long time. I learnt only that he had married suddenly. If so, I assumed he must have dispensed with Sarana's services.

I had to go to Kandy again one *Wesak* night in order to record a programme of carols which were to be sung from a boat on the lake. On that occasion I telephoned Van der Bona from Kandy.

'What's this I hear? So you did it all very secretly without informing any of us! . . . However, I'm very happy indeed,' I said congratulating him on his marriage.

'I didn't want to bother other people. But when are you coming this way again? Do come and stay as you used to do in the old days. Bring your wife along, too, now that I'm no longer a bachelor. Kusuma is also anxious to meet you.' I realised on hearing the name that he had married a Sinhalese woman. It was probably a further step motivated by his conscious or perhaps unconscious desire to 'belong' to the Sinhalese race, I thought.

'It's a little difficult to come today. I came up to record a programme of *Wesak* carols. I must get back tonight. I'll take three or four days' leave and come up another time with the family.'

'Can't you drop in on your way down to Colombo tonight? Come and see Sarana. He's our family astrologer now. What time do you expect to finish your work?'

'About eight or nine tonight. I had intended to go straight down to Colombo.' Van der Bona's story that Sarana had become an astrologer aroused my curiosity. 'Why don't you come here instead, and stay here tonight? You can visit Sarana in the morning.'

'Why, is Sarana not living with you?'

'No, but he lives close by. I'll tell you all about it.'

It was about ten that night when I finished the radio programme and reached Galaha. Van der Bona and his wife had kept dinner for me. Van der Bona's wife, though she spoke faultless English, appeared to me to have been brought up in a traditional Sinhalese home. It was clear she was soon to be a mother.

There was a new servant in a white tunic coat to serve at table. A middle-aged fat woman was laying out the dishes in the pantry.

I was about to ask for news of Sarana when Van der Bona brought up the topic. 'I've sent a message to Sarana to come over tomorrow. He lives close by. Sometimes he spends the night here in the garage.'

'What did you mean when you said he was the family astrologer? I didn't quite understand that.'

Van der Bona looked at his wife.

'Ask Kusuma. She can't do without him. She consults him about auspicious times, horoscopes, good and bad periods, there's no end to it. He has already predicted the date and time of our child's birth. It will be a daughter he says.'

'Then you don't need to consult a doctor,' I said laughing.

'George is exaggerating. However, the man does make accurate predictions,' said Kusuma slightly embarrassed.

'Why, you consult Sarana before taking any important step nowadays, don't you? It was he who chose an auspicious day for our wedding, an auspicious time to leave the house, and numerous other things when we returned home. This year we celebrated New Year in traditional Sinhalese style under Sarana's instructions.'

Van der Bona's mental make-up was now quite clear to me. However, Sarana's transformation I could not figure out.

About seven the next morning I heard someone knock at my door. I got up and opened it. It took me a minute or two to recognize that it was Sarana who was standing outside. Seeing his withered wasted appearance I was overcome with a sudden surge of sympathy for him. Most of his hair was grey. His front teeth were drawn and seemed to shake as he spoke.

'How are you Sarana? I didn't recognize you. You've grown quite thin. Have you been ill?'

'No, thank heaven, I've been quite well. I now have a little shrine of my own, you know.'

'A shrine?'

'Yes, close by here.' His eyes grew big as in the old days but their light had dimmed.

'Where is it?'

'As you come up the hill by the roadside there is that big *Bo* tree. Just there. You must have seen it.'

About a quarter of a mile away, at the entrance to the tea estate, there was a *Bo* tree of which I was aware. I faintly remembered having seen a statue of Buddha and a little stone altar on which villagers offered flowers and incense. But I had not known that there was also a shrine there for the gods.

'So, what is it you do there?'

'I am the priest of the shrine. Would you like to see the place, sir?'

I washed, dressed, left a message for Van der Bona that I would be back soon, and accompanied Sarana.

'Many people come to the shrine even from places as far away as Paingomuwa. The place has considerable magical properties,' he said as we walked. 'Ask the lady of the house what she thinks about it. I have obtained many divine favours for her, too. Recently her sister succeeded in getting a job. She was chosen from among two hundred and sixty others.'

We arrived at the *Bo* tree and walked around behind its enormous trunk. Not far from the altar was a steep precipice. On one side of the cliff was a stone slab about five feet long and three feet wide. The slab seemed intended to cover something. At one end of it was a fissure not more than a foot wide. Sarana put his feet into this opening, slowly slipped through and disappeared. I was wondering what I should do when I heard his voice from under the ground.

'Get in sir, it's not difficult. Put your feet in first and then slowly lower yourself down.'

Following his instructions I lowered myself into the ground. It was not as deep as I had imagined. Inside was a rock cave with barely enough standing room. I could see nothing. Just then Sarana struck a match and lit a little oil lamp which was on an abutment in the rock wall. A bottle of coconut oil was on the ground just below it. Sarana spoke squatting, and I, too, squatted beside him listening to what he was saying. 'This place is sacred to god Irugalbandara. However, the gods Dedimunda, Viramnunda, Saman, Vibiisana, Katharagama all cast their beneficent glances on this place. If one makes a vow here and then invokes the gods for three continuous sessions—that is, one-and-a-half days—after seven days the request will be granted. One can curse people too. Many such instances have been successful. If there's anything you particularly want, sir, let me know.'

I though I heard a rustling sound and turned round. To the right of me was a crack in the rock. It was half blocked with dirt.

'There is a tunnel there. It goes for miles underground and comes out at the Temple of the Tooth in Kandy.'

Since I did not believe what Sarana said, I observed the crack a little more closely. A huge snake dragged itself out as I watched and came towards us. I jumped up, trying to get out.

'Wait, wait, don't be frightened. He won't harm us,' said Saṛana in a whisper.

The cobra raised its head, puffed up its hood as if to observe us, then lowered his head again, turned and went out through the fissure. 'The snake is the guardian of this place.'

'Aren't you afraid to stay inside here with that thing there?'

'No. He will not harm me. I wouldn't be able to carry on this work here without him.' I became aware that Sarana respectfully referred to the snake as a person, 'him,' not a thing which was how I referred to it.

I had no mind to stay in there any longer. My whole body was covered in sweat. My arms and feet were numb.

'Well, I'll come another time and see you,' I said, getting up to leave.

'If you make a vow to offer a certain number of baskets of flowers, or light a number of lamps, and then tell me what it is you want . . .'

'Good, good,' I said extricating my head with difficulty and climbing out. Sarana walked with me to Van der Bona's house. I could not make out what in the world had motivated him to take to this particular profession.

Although I disliked doing so I was tempted to ask him a direct question.

'How is your wife, Sarana? Where do you live now?'

'She wants to end our marriage now. I will never allow that. I'll teach her a lesson. Every day I invoke curses on her before the gods. I shall destroy her. My curses will strike her, and the child too.'

'Why does she want to end the marriage?' I asked, rather taken aback.

'She wants a divorce but as long as I live I will not allow it.'

He continued to mutter to himself as if he had not heard my question.

'They are all like that—the bastards. They promise women that they will make them film stars and then put them in trouble. That woman—she's a tough customer. She very nearly got me into a trap . . . I barely escaped. The gods showed me this place in a dream. I hear she is now in Colombo. That bastard will never marry her, though he now says he will. If I divorce her he will marry her, she says. He's a married man . . . how can he marry her . . . I will bring her crawling to me on her knees.'

Van der Bona and his wife were waiting for me for breakfast.

'What has really happened to Sarana? Whom is he cursing all the time?' I asked.

Van der Bona laughed. 'The man says he has a shrine somewhere around here.'

'Yes, I saw it. In fact I went in, right in under the ground.'

'Really! He's been asking me to come, too, but I haven't gone yet. He sleeps in that little thatched hut beyond the *Bo* tree. I keep telling him to come and sleep here.'

'Where is his wife, then?'

'His wife? Ah yes, the man married without even telling me. How did you come to know about it?'

'He told me of it at the time.

'Is that so? That woman truly fooled him. I found out the details later. You must know him, that film director Devarajan. Well, he had been keeping this woman as his mistress and probably got tired of her and sent her off. I don't know very much about that part of it. But it was obviously when she was about to have a child that she caught this fool of ours. She got herself married to Sarana before the child was born, whether for reasons of shame or for support for the child I do not know. Thats what happened when you were here last. When he heard she had had a child, that fellow went to the hospital. Yes— Devarajan. It was the day Sarana met him there that he tried to commit suicide.'

'So Devarajan has taken the woman back?'

'Yes, she now lives somewhere or other with the child. Veluppillai told me. The man plans to marry her, I hear. That's why there is all this talk about a divorce. Sarana must have told you about it.'

I was tempted to tell Van der Bona to his face that it was he who was responsible for all that had happened to Sarana. But how could I say it in front of his wife? It was difficult to imagine that he hadn't realized it himself. However, since it had not been done intentionally I felt I should not blame him too much.

'Where did the man learn to make predictions?' I asked.

'I don't know where he learned the art, but his predictions are certainly very accurate,' said Kusuma. 'Sarana says it's a special power from the gods.'

However educated Van der Bona may have been, it was obvious that he also believed in such things. Or was it that he felt such belief was essential in order to appear more completely Sinhalese?

As for Sarana, when one considers the full extent of his terrible unhappiness, one is grateful for any illusion that might console him and give him the will to continue living.

—Translated by Ranjini Obeysekere

THE CART

It was the police driver who drove the cart into the police station that was fortified with a barbed wire fence and had sand bags round it. Those who saw him driving the cart in his police uniform suppressed their laughter at the incongruity of the situation with difficulty. They turned their eyes away only out of fear. But the policeman on duty with a rifle in hand couldn't help himself and cracked into spontaneous laughter. The driver drove on regardless without protest and with his head bowed down because he was still the driver despite his police uniform. When he walked into the police station having unyoked the bullock and tied it to the cart wheel he saw that the carter was still being questioned. He looked at him for a moment and then at the cart and the bullock as if to convince himself that it was the same carter.

'Name?' 'Ranasinghe.'

'Age?' '44.'

The Cart

'Occupation?' 'Carter.'

'Married?' 'No.'

'Home?' 'The cart.'

'I'm asking you where you were born?' 'Born in Divullewe but living in the cart.'

'Have you gone to school?' 'Yes.'

'Up to which grade?' 'Passed the Senior.'

The Policeman paused as he studied the suspect discreetly. He looked at his thick black curly hair and the beard that had grown from his face down to his waist. He saw the random streaks of white hair that had occasionally sneaked out from the rest and he also saw his betel-stained teeth that were wearing out. He noticed too that his small, sharp and somewhat sunken eyes were directed at his official badge.

'With this kind of education why didn't you go for a job at the time?' 'Well, I have a job.'

'I mean a job that suits your education.' 'Is there any thing like that . . . a job that suits one's education?'

The constable who hadn't expected this kind of answer slapped him hard, twice across the face, with the pen still held between his fingers. The carter took the blows easily and his small half-sunken eyes devoid of any emotion were still directed at the official badge. The constable thought that he would pick up the ball-point pen that fell, but he didn't. He eyed him for a moment and then, like someone possessed, suddenly rose and held him by the hair with both hands. He shook him violently a few times and made him stand.

> 'Remember . . . you have to answer only what I ask you. If you love your life, don't try to be too smart . . . We don't want a display of your education here . . . . Better remember where you are now.'

The carter looked on—a vacant incomprehensible look written all over his face. Meanwhile the constable who got up as if to go away picked up the pen that had fallen and returned to his seat where he settled himself comfortably again. He thought for a while before his next question. Tension and anger were mounting in him due to his own lack of experience with cross-examinations. Moreover, here before him was a man whose answers were never the standard ones. He looked at the carter's face before asking the next question. With his hair now dishevelled the carter seemed to look taller than his usual six feet. His broad shoulders, the beard with a touch of grey here and there, the sharp eyes directed towards him and the long slim hands instilled a certain amount of fear in the constable.

The constable placed the pen on the open page and closed his book, then he rose and walked away without looking at him. The carter was still standing there. He saw the old jeep parked in front of the police station and his own cart a little beyond it. The bullock was tied to the cart wheel and there was saliva dripping from its mouth. The next moment these images seemed to melt away before him. People with turbanned heads walked briskly past the police station. Stooping slightly, without casting an eye in that direction.

'My job is good enough for me but for some one else it is not so . . . . Does any one have a job to match his education? I have passed my Senior well with English Language and Literature too as subjects. With Tamil businessman I converse in Tamil. My school mate Gunaratne is now a lecturer in an American university, I who solved mathematical problems all day long on demy paper, am still a carter. The issue is not about the suitability of my job but about how each person is ultimately destined for his particular profession.'

'Alright, now sit down and answer my questions.'

The carter felt as if the constable's rough voice and tough demeanour had abandoned him for a moment. He couldn't really comprehend why he was now wearing his cap. Could it be an official regulation? A while ago it just rested on the table. When the constable saw confidence with which the carter sat down on the bench and the way he stooped towards him with his hands placed on the table, he felt as if he was the one going to be interrogated. He wanted to order him to take his hands of the table but he didn't. He opened the book once again to remind himself of his last question.

'Who are your closest friends?' 'The bullock and the dog.'

'Who did you say, you donkey?' 'The bullock that pulls the cart and the dog that lives in the gunny' rack.'

The constable got up. He circled the long table in long swift strides and came from behind, unnerving the carter who was now looking back. Suddenly the carter felt as if a huge vice tightened its cruel grip round his elbows. Before he had time to think, he was dragged over the short wall into the sitting room. He was dragged so swiftly and strongly that a few bits of plaster from the wall came down when his hip knocked the wall. The next moment a heavy thundering slap landed on his cheek. It was a slap no ordinary man could take, coming from the constable's right hand, powered by an expansive circular movement. But he was expecting it. Despite the pain in his hip, he leaned backwards a few degree and avoided it. The constable who lost his balance as a consequence, slipped and fell, his head striking the ground. He lay there, like an animal, bent down, with his hands pressed on the ground, and from under them with his face upturned he looked at the carter. While still rubbing his painful hip with his right hand, the carter twisted his head round and watched the constable behind him. At that moment another constable walked into the room rubbing his palms together and whistling a tune to himself. Almost by instinct he seemed to have understood what was going on.

'Shall I give him the works, friend?' he asked his comrade as he twisted one of carter's arms and pushed him hard and far. The first constable who was up and ready by now, kicked him hard in the groin. The carter was thrown back, the constable bent forward, clapped his hands, jumped and punched him on the face. His weather-beaten, dark and slightly emaciated cheek swelled. As the carter tried to assess the damage by running the middle finger of his right hand along his cheek, he received another kick, in the stomach. This time he fell, sprawling on the ground, like a falling tree.

When he regained consciousness, he was back in his cell. An unbearable urge to urinate and a pain as if his rib cage had been blown into smithereens made him feel miserable. He also felt an unquenchable thirst. For some reason a few tears welled into his eyes. He bent his head down with difficulty and wiped his eyes and forehead.

He heard the noise of police jeeps leaving and returning to base. He also heard the crunch of boots on the cement floor and later someone whistling. An ominous silence followed. He remembered the bullock, the dog and the cart. Squatting on the floor and holding on to the iron bars of the cell, he raised himself slowly to look at the road over the short wall and the police table near it. The bullock with its raised head had the same vacant look in its eyes as it still stood in the same posture as before. The shafts of the cart were pushed down which made him feel as if the rear of the cart was raised unusually high. He wondered whether the shafts were broken. He reasoned out that it was a pillar in the portico that blocked his view which gave this comic appearance to the cart as if it were broken in two. A few more days like this and the shaft of the cart would be eaten by termites. He would be taken for questioning any time now and then he would tell them that the bullock and the dog needed to be fed and given water. The dog must still be sleeping in the gunny rack under the cart, he thought. But no one came to question him in the afternoon. The number of people that were brought to the police station in jeeps from time to time, increased steadily. There were also those who came to the police station and surrendered themselves voluntarily. Two others were put into his cell. The constable who pushed them inside and locked up the cell went away without even looking at him.

In the evening it was to the room of the Officer-in-Charge that he was taken for questioning. There was another policeman in civil dress in the room along with the OIC. Questioning started after the two officers summarized their points about him between them in English. The carter informed them that the bullock and the dog had to be fed and given water. A constable was summoned and given orders to do so. They heard the passing comments of the constable as he left them:

So it has now become our job to feed and give water to cattle and dogs too, eh!

But they pretended not to hear him.

'Did you cook for the terrorists that night?' 'I cooked for a few. I do not know whether they were terrorists or not.'

'Why did you feel like cooking for them?' 'I was getting ready to cook for the evening. They too wanted some thing cooked. My pots and pans were very small. They brought big ones. I cooked and they helped.'

'You didn't know any of them earlier?' 'No.'

'Is it usual for you to cook for strangers?' 'I give food not only to a hungry man but even to an animal if I can afford it.'

'That was not your house. Was it?' 'I have no house. The seven days of the week I spend in seven places. In the evening I unload the goods at one fair and again the following evening at the end of the fair I load them to take them to the next fair.'

'Why did they come specially in search of you too cook their food?' 'That I don't know. On Saturdays I go near the stream. I bathe my bullock and dog too. It's a nice shady place, more comfortable than a house. It's on a Saturday that I oil the cart wheels and apply margosa oil to the bullock's horns and its forehead to keep away the flies. By then I get very hungry. Cooking alone for one man is tedious but if there is some one to talk to then you won't feel it.'

'With whom do you talk after that?' 'With the bullock and the dog.'

'In what language?' 'I speak any language that comes

The Cart

to my mouth at the moment. They don't need a language like us—they understand from the way you talk to them. The dog knows when I order it to bathe. Of course, it doesn't run straight to the river and start to bathe. When I order it to bathe, it starts running in the opposite direction. Then I have to shout out loud in filth and block its path a bit and the fellow run straight into the water. It's the same with the bullock too.'

'When you're free you must be reading books and magazines too?' 'It's useless. Absolutely useless. I just read bits of newspapers whenever I got hold of them.'

'If there is any thing on politics?' 'No, I read just about anything that would help me to remember the alphabet.'

The two officers conversed in English and decided that he was apparently no fool and that the best thing would be to hold an identification parade.

'Upto what grade have you studied?'

He answered in English selecting his words and articulating them carefully. He explained that he got through his Senior and that for some time he had studied in the English medium too. He added that he could speak Tamil as well though he had now forgotten its written script. Because he had not used English for quite some time and because of the coarseness of his mouth due to excessive chewing of betel, he felt as if the words rolled in his mouth before he could finally blurt them out.

A long silence followed. Leaning against the backs of the chair the two officers became pensive. They didn't look at each other. After some time the officer in civils heaved a long sigh and suggested in Sinhala that they should perhaps hold the identification parade and finish it off.

A constable lined up about seven or eight young men. Among them were bearded ones as well as young lads who appeared to have hardly passed their early adolescence. But two things were common to all. One was the eyebrows, noses and lips of each one were swollen, cracked, bloodstained and disfigured. The other was that none of them looked particularly well-nourished.

'Is there any one here who ate with you that day?'

He studied the faces before him for a moment. Even if he recognized anyone should he tell them so? He had never been the nosy type, one who would painstakingly delve into the personal affairs of others. He believed that it was none of his business. To him everybody was equal.

'So you don't know any one here? . . . . Okay, go and put him back in his cell.' The constables almost dragged him along as they pushed him back into the cell. The two men with dark and puffed-up faces who were leaning against the wall in a corner of the cell almost rose to their feet in their sleep. But soon they went back to their world of sleep. With the need to urinate and his chest and ribs hurting so much, he thought that he might pass into unconsciousness at any moment. The numerous sounds, the lamenting that rent the air and the gun shots heard at various times in the night disturbed his sleep. In one on two days, however, he had learnt to take the hunger, the thirst, the fool smells, lamenting and rude talk as the accepted things of the day.

How would nice it be if one can forget all these and think of some thing more pleasant, some thing more positive! Today I'm compelled to urinate here but even my dog urinates only after walking to an acceptable distance and ensuring my approval for the act. My bullock never passes urine or dung in the water. It finishes both these acts before I lead it into the water for its bath. For some time now I've been living a rather tranquil and uneventful life, almost coming to terms with life in my own way. The need never arose for me to think deeply or seriously of anything nor did I have any occasion for regrets for that matter. During these quiet years the whole world to me has been the places and the things that I passed every week on my way—the paddy fields, the bridges, the culverts, the buffalo herds that wallowed in the mud, the flocks of cranes and parrots that flew free and high over the paddy fields, the sprawling acres of tall teak, the mountains of Tissawa and Dematawa clothed in ashen clouds and of course the sun and the wind and the rain. My bullock and the dog are my friends. Most of my conversations have been with my bullock. I recite verses to him; I sing folk songs to him.

In the midst of his reverie he remembered his bullock. He thought that he would need to polish and shine the brass caps that embellished its horns. He would need to fit new shoes to its feet—a painful process for the poor fellow, since every time its feet were shod it had to lie on the ground, flat on his side. Nevertheless you had to do it or else it would slip and fall and break its legs. There is no single answer to the problem: the only way out is to fix its shoes only when the old ones were too worn out for further use. In the afternoon a constable came and took him out of the cell.

'You fellow, where are you from, man?'

Once in trying to sort out where I lived they broke my ribs. In the book it has been recorded that I was born in Divullewa. Now again they want to know where I live. Whoever asks a question, does so to get the answer of his own choice. The truth beyond it, is not palatable.

'What's your village, fellow?' 'Divullewe . . . . *Ralahamy* bullock!'

'You donkey, though you have time to look after

your animals do you think that we too can do the same? Now tell me the names of two people who know you.'
'My elder brother Mr. Gunasinghe'
'One more name . . . the Gramasevaka?' 'I don't know the Gramasevaka. I know the old Headman.'

He was bundled into the back of the jeep. In front were the two officers who had questioned him. The constable who accompanied him at the back was well armed. Following the directions of the carter, the vehicle passed through the countryside—past trees, past the scrub jungle and past the graveyards.

It stopped finally when they reached his brother's compound. His brother walked towards them, chewing the last bit of betel quid in his mouth and looked at him straight and unhesitatingly.

'Who is this?' 'My younger brother.'
'Have you got his belongings here? . . . his books, papers and so on?' 'Yes.'

He brought out a fairly large trunk containing his possessions. He was asked to open it himself. The carter was immediately transported to the realms of his childhood. This was the box that he carried to his school boarding-house. He sniffed and bent down to feel whether it still had the loving old aroma distilled from the smell of the new books and clothes and soap and powder that were packed into it.

The books and various papers were examined carefully each one separately. Right on top were a few bundles of red monitor's exercise books, a few bundles of English and Sinhala books and a few Tamil poetry booklets. The constable examined each one of them. When he saw the pictures of two bearded men on two book covers he took them immediately into his custody. He wiped the dust out of them carefully with the sleeve of his own coat and placed them in the hands of his superior. Those were the pictures of Shakespeare's Macbeth and Rabindranath Tagore.

'So, you were a drama man those days eh!' 'Those were the books that we had to study at the time.'

Under them was a large hand-sewn book made of demy paper. This was the book in which he used to solve mathematical problems for practice. Under it was a large envelope with the governmental insignia on it. His sports certificates and the Senior School Certificate were in it. The constable who took the envelope carefully, dusted in twice flicking it with his index finger, before he handed it over to the OIC. Except for its brown lacquer seal, the rest of it was mostly moth-eaten.

'When you think of the times he could have got a good job then,' the OIC confided to the other officer in English. It was almost a whisper.

'That's right, sir.'

The two officers were surprised by the villagers response to their conversation. The villager with his sunburnt scaly skin and betel—stained mouth was slightly balding in the front. He had applied oil liberally to his head and this gave it a little shine too. He looked on vacantly, absolutely devoid of any emotion. However, his tongue was active, almost disobediently exploring the nooks and corners of his mouth in search of the last remnants of the betel quid that were still hidden somewhere there.

'What's your job?' 'Cultivator.'

The carter was put back into the jeep. The two brothers did not talk to each other. The elder brother watched the jeep disappearing in the distance and said

'He'll never do anything wrong', as he walked back into the house.

Early next morning a few groups of armed police men left the station. The suspects were removed to another place in a few private vehicles. By noon a few more people came to the police station and surrendered themselves voluntarily. Each one was given a kick on the back before being pushed into a cell and locked up.

Not even a drop of water was give to anyone until evening. The forlorn silence was broken only by the arrival of sarong-clad volunteers. They sat on the short wall and smoked and boasted late into the night. In the meantime the constable came announcing:

The fool was asked to be released today . . . . I nearly forgot that.

He then opened the cell door and shouted, 'Now for god's sake get the hell out of here, you fellow. You can go anywhere you like.'

The carter slowly raised himself to a squatting position. Placing his hands on his knees he stood up and gazed at the road for a moment. His cart was still there in the blazing sun.

'Ralahamy, my bullock?'

'Is there any other bullock other than you. At least now get the hell out of here if you love your life. You have given us enough trouble. I warn you, there is only one more hour for the curfew . . . you understand?'

The volunteers were smoking and chatting their time away merrily. He didn't understand a word of what they said nor did he care to. His thoughts were with his bullock. The thought came to him that it could be grazing somewhere behind the police station, raising its head from time to time to see whether he was walking towards it. At the same time he felt sad with the intruding thought that the bullock must have been uncared for and grown weaker and thinner in the last few days. The next moment again this sadness gave way to a new feeling of exhilaration accompanied by the thought that today, once again, both of them would be returning to their familiar everyday word.

'Are you going away or do you want to get back to your cell again?'

'To go away, I want my bullock back.'

'Can't a bullock like you pull that cart along man? . . . when you see what's happening to people around you, can't you understand what can happen to a bullock?'

The volunteers broke into laughter, clapping their hands too. The carter seemed to be oblivious to every thing that was happening around. The eyes in his darkened swollen face seemed to grow narrower. With long strides, like some animal stalking its prey, he walked towards the constable. The constable eyed him steadily and started retreating towards the machine gun that was lying on the table. In one fleeting moment the carter's right hand moved and the constable was dragged towards him as by a magic wand! He was caught by his elbow and turned around before being pushed away hard to fall down at the foot of the short wall and lie against it. The short machine gun was not familiar to the carter's hand but he loved its almost dainty look. When he was a school cadet, he remembered that he had never aimed a gun at any living thing, just the target on the mound of earth.

— *Translated by A.T. Dharmapriya*

Part Three:
Stories from the Tamil

Contents

A Basket of Shoots   181
    N.S.M. Ramaiah (1961)

Black Magic and Nostalgia   192
    A. Santhan (1976)

Night Bird   199
    A. Santhan (1974)

Release   204
    Shanmugam Sivalingam

A Basket of Shoots

Letchumi was standing in a queue waiting for instructions on the day's work.

'Sister, where do I work today?' she asked, looking in the direction of the women who stood there in small groups. Letchumi slung the empty basket over her shoulder and held the strap in her left hand. There was no response to her innocuous inquiry. On other days, many would have volunteered to assist her. They would have said, 'Come, dear. You can work with us in our rows.' Today they seemed hostile. Letchumi was a vivacious lass. Her captivating smile would reveal her beautiful teeth which gleamed like white rice. She was charming, and the women living on the hills liked her.

But a cold reception confronted her. Her companions averted their faces as if from an enemy. 'What is the matter with you today?' she snapped and turned towards the old *kankani* (supervisor). He was well disposed towards her and usually welcomed her warmly with a toothless smile.

She spoke, '*kankani Appachi*, my . . .' But even before she could come to the point, he bawled out, 'So here comes her ladyship. Has it dawned only now? You are late, aren't you? How can I give you work? The boss will pounce on me if I do. How will I answer him?'

Letchumi was deeply hurt by his harsh words, coming as they did, the first thing in the morning. A poor tea-plucker on an estate cannot show her anger, however provoked, to an accountant or a supervisor. If she did—there would be no escape—she would have to quit. Concealing her resentment, she said, 'Please, sir don't scold me. I thought the other girls would come early to get their assignments and that they would have got mine too. I can't understand them.'

The old man raised his voice and said angrily, 'After what you have done, do you really expect them to help you?' He shouted impatiently, 'Go . . . get lost . . . go to the far end of the hill.'

Letchumi took the empty basket from the floor, swung it across her shoulder and walked reluctantly to the end of the hill. Neither the basket nor the rough apron cloth could conceal the beauty of her youthful gait.

Pluckers who are intent on getting poundage, do not frequent either the top, the front or the back rows far down the hill. In the top section, there are frequently a number of irregular, short and incomplete rows and a plucker has to climb up and down a thousand times. The women who work in the rear, are usually women with babies or the sluggish and the old. They walk slowly as if in a solemn procession. It is hard to deal with them. They often pass their load to the young women to carry and sometimes even to get it weighed. For this reason, young workers do not come this way. Letchumi's lively nature, her beauty and her ways gave her a unique advantage over the simple, nondescript, ordinary women of the estate. They always sought her company. But today it was different. The older women wondered why Letchumi was hounded out and set to work on this desolate patch.

Letchumi was at a loss as to what had happened. She could not guess the reason. Their apathy pained her. She thought about it again and again. She stood in the back row. The very last row on all those hills. Slighted and rejected by all her friends, she felt dejected. An uneasy loneliness gripped her heart.

Letchumi tied the apron around her waist and fastened it with a black rope. She tucked her saree up to her knees in order to prevent the bushes from tearing its hem. She then tied a kerchief around her head and adjusted it so that it did not smudge the two streaks of holy ash on her forehead. She was ready for work.

An old woman plucking tea nearby, noticed Letchumi. 'How come the wind is blowing in this direction! You do not usually work here. What happened?' she asked. Letchumi was in a sombre mood. She did not wish to talk. She said, 'Nothing special,' hoping to end the conversation. The old woman was in a mood to chat. 'You are not one to come this way without a compelling reason. Tell me what really happened,' she pressed.

Letchumi was annoyed. She said, 'I swear there was nothing!'

The old woman said, 'Come on, there is no need to swear early in the morning!'

Letchumi reverentially touched the tea bush and silently started plucking the tender shoots that were drenched in mist. Soon both her hands were full of shoots. She examined them; they seemed good. She turned towards the old woman who was picking shoots laboriously one by one. It was a cold frosty morning and her hands were shivering. Letchumi asked her to chant the prayer for a good harvest that day. The old woman intoned '*Poli! Poli! Shanmukha poli!*' It was a prayer to Lord Skanda to swell the basket with shoots.

Letchumi's hands worked with great speed. In March the tea bushes are a lush green—a magnificent sight. For the expert, tea-plucking is a heady, blissful game. It should have been so for Letchumi too; the shoots were breaking fast in her hands. But she experienced no such ecstatic exuberance. The indifference of her friends, their strange silence, gnawed at her heart. The reason for their behaviour came out when they all assembled for the evening session of weighing the shoots.

At four o'clock when the siren sounded, all the pluckers descended from the hills and assembled in front of the store. In the sweltering heat of the afternoon sun, Letchumi put the basket down and wiped her face with a kerchief. Spreading out all the fingers of her hand, she pressed the swelling tea shoots down hard in her basket.

When the *kankani* was satisfied that all had come, he went to the hunchbacked accountant and said haltingly, 'Shall we start weighing?'

The accountant who was peering at the check-roll cast his eyes on the labour force waiting outside. They were standing in a line with their baskets. He stepped on to the gunny sack carpet. The weighing bridge was brought and also the weighing tray. Four women took their places in the weighing area; their job was to hold the beam and load the trays. Everything was ready. The weighing had to start. The accountant took a step forward as if something important had just crossed his mind. His gait, his stance and the manner in which he looked at the workers were calculated to give the impression of a white sahib who by some quirk of fate had been born among the dark-skinned Tamils. He could not speak good Tamil either. With great difficulty, he managed to speak Tamil haltingly with a European accent, like some white planter. Most people would have laughed at his

A Basket of Shoots

behaviour. But these were simple estate workers. Some young officers took pride in strutting about in this style.

He looked scornfully at them. His eyes which were assessing the situation, ran from right to left along the lines of workers and stopped for a while on reaching Letchumi. He looked at her from head to foot and proceeded to the very end of the line. Then he turned in the direction of the *kankani* and called out to him. The *kankani* who had been watching the movements of the Accountant closely, came forward. Why the *kankani* adulated the Accountant and bent in half before him was a mystery no one could understand. 'Call Letchumi here,' he said. The supervisor understood the problem. He looked at Letchumi with sympathy, but raised his voice and shouted:

'Here, girl! Come here. The boss wants to speak to you.'

Letchumi's insides rose up to her heart and dropped in sheer fright.

'Is it me?' she asked.

'Yes, it's you.'

Letchumi's limps quivered in fear. 'What sorrow is this?' Her face, burnt in the midday heat, shrivelled now in fear.

She stood in front of the huge crowd, feeling herself shrink in shame and fear.

The *kankani* was pensively drawing circles on the ground with his right toe. He glanced at Letchumi.

She stood with head bowed.

'Letchumi'

'Sir?' She raised her eyes half-way and looked down again.

'Four or five days back, you plucked tea on hill number twenty-four. How many pounds did you pluck per hour?' Then, as if he had just remembered, he said, 'Ah! yes, fifty-seven pounds!'

'Fifty-seven pounds, sir' said Letchumi. 'Was it fifty-seven pounds? In fact, I cannot remember. But there are many here who can.'

He cast a grave look at those in front of him.

'Letchumi, can you once more demonstrate your ability to pluck fifty-seven pounds of tea between nine o'clock and one o'clock?'

Letchumi's eyebrows curved questioningly.

'Fifty-seven pounds again? What for?'

She turned towards the *kankani*. '*Appachi*, why this request?' she asked softly.

'How do I know? Ask the boss yourself.'

How could she summon the courage to question him?

The accountant himself came forward and said, 'Letchumi, you are well aware that matters concerning women can affect us. Besides. I am a bachelor. If rumours spread, my superiors may believe them. There are fifteen experienced workers on this estate who were in service before you and who can pluck better than you. You joined only last year. They suspect your claim of having plucked fifty-seven pounds. No one has complained so far. But I hear they are talking among themselves.'

The *kankani* noticed that the talk was becoming rather unpleasant. He said, 'It is good to forget it. Leave it alone.'

'No, *kankani*! I must talk about it. Perhaps there is no need for a public inquiry. This matter concerns me. I wish to be frank about it. That Letchumi is a relative of mine adds to the problem. I want to be open and frank regarding this matter. Letchumi, I believe you understand my problem. Can you pluck that quantity again and demonstrate you abilities?'

Suddenly she lifted her bowed head, stood erect and looked boldly at the *kankani*, the accountant and the crowd. If a sleeping tigress had been poked in the ribs, it would have snarled like her.

'Come on, child, why that hard look? Give your answer to the accountant.'

What could she say? The accountant had hinted at some deception. Keeping silent would not remove the slur. So she looked the accountant straight in the eye and said, 'Who said it is not possible? I can pluck. I will demonstrate my ability to pluck that amount.'

She looked down to hide the tears that streamed and flowed down her cheeks as a rat-snake slides down hill.

The assembled workers watched the proceedings in silence. Though they were interested in the turn of events and anxious to know how matters would shape up, they assumed a calm and docile appearance and stood passively like a herd of cattle.

In general, the estate women had this strange mentality. They would never antagonize the accountant or the *kankani* out of fear, but they would use other strategies to see that their grievances reached the ears of the officers. When matters came to light, they would feign ignorance with innocence written on their faces, they would say, 'O God! Some horrible woman has spread unjust rumours.'

The accountant looked at the congregated crowd and said, 'I am very pleased, Letchumi. You say you can repeat your performance, good. That is up to you.' Looking penetratingly at her, he said, 'You must do it. If you don't, I will have to be very harsh with you'

Letchumi wiped her face with her scarf. What had happened was not a threat; nor was it a vengeful act. It was a challenge to her integrity.

*

A small oil lamp made of tin had been lit. Arumukam bent forward and blew the embers in the fireplace. The cinders started glowing. Then he picked up some twigs broken from a dried tea bush, broke them into small pieces and put them into the fire. It burned bright. Warming his hands over the fire, Arumukam looked at Letchumi. She was looking intently at him, waiting for his comments.

Sitting close to the fire, he asked her, 'So what are you going to do?'

The yellows and reds of the fire were painting her face in their varied colours.

'With great aplomb, you spoke arrogantly in the midst of that crowd. That is not enough. You will have to fulfil your promise. Can you do it?'

Seated against the wall with her right leg bent, she looked at him and smiled. 'Would I have made that pledge, had I thought it impossible?'

'You can do it. My foot! That day on my way for lunch, I plucked some shoots while talking to you. But for my contribution you could not have got fifty-seven pounds.'

He was betrothed to her, her future husband. In the evenings, when Arumukam visited them, he would speak to all in general for a while and then spend some time alone with Letchumi. At such times, Letchumi's parents would discretely move out and attend to their chores. After speaking a few words with her, Arumukam, unlike others, would not go away impelled by some sense of false dignity. He and she would discuss family problems and problems that arose in their work place till about seven-thirty or eight o'clock and then, he would go to his line room. At a time when they should forget the world and speak of love to each other . . . pressing economic problems confronted them. Food and job-related questions occupied their minds. This problem of the fifty-seven pounds of tea had been brought about by him. Men would usually finish their work by one o'clock. There were a few who were in the good books of the supervisor, so they had the courage to leave by noon. Arumukam was one of them. One day when he left early for lunch, he saw Letchumi plucking shoots alone by the side of a hill. He thought he would have a chat with her, and while speaking to her, he too had started plucking shoots. Hands used to work, cannot be idle. The tongue keeps talking and the hands keep working. This goes on till death. The extra shoots that he plucked were responsible for the enormous weight of fifty-seven pounds and was the cause of enormous problems.

'I have an idea. Shall I come at noon and pick some shoots for you,' Arumukam suggested.

'Oh no!' she cried. 'Everybody's eyes will be on me. Another person helping is an offence. But now it will be a crime.' Holding her cheeks in both hands, she shook her head. 'We have no need for more problems.'

'What else can be done?' he asked in a troubled voice.

'I will pluck as much as I can. If I fail, I will accept my dismissal and go to another hill. If I stay, they will suspect the accountant.'

With a sigh, Arumukam stood up. 'Do as you please,' he said with resignation. Taking the muffler from his shoulder, he tied it turban-wise round his head and left.

Letchumi's mother who was seated in the verandah, stood up respectfully to let her future son-in-law pass by. 'Did you give him tea?' she asked as she entered the house.

'Yes, mother. He took his tea before leaving,' said Letchumi.

The dog, half asleep at the entrance, barked twice on seeing Arumukam, but stopped when it recognized him as their usual visitor.

*

It was one o'clock. The plucked shoots were being

weighed. That was a hill with a good crop of young shoots. Therefore, many continued to pluck without going for lunch. Forty, fifty, the pounds kept increasing quickly. In the baskets, the young shoots had risen to the height of a man. The women who hold the sacks and those who press them in, were standing by. The queue that had formed to get the shoots weighed, was moving slowly. It was Letchumi's turn. The sackman lifted Letchumi's basket. It felt heavy, like a rock. He lifted it by putting his hand at the bottom of the basket and tried to empty the contents into the weighing tray. Nothing fell on the tray. Trampling had compressed the shoots like cement. According to the usual procedure, he kicked the open end of the basket twice and shook it four or five times. The shoots became disentangled and started tumbling down. The tray got filled and the shoots rose as high as the pinnacle of a temple. Letchumi turned round and looked at the accountant.

The boss looked at the immense heap of young shoots. 'Are these shoots?' he asked. 'They are mature leaves and stems. It is not proper to pluck these. Call the supervisor.'

'Supervisor, are these shoots? Did you ask Letchumi to pluck today?'

'Yes, Sir. She came after the nine o'clock weighing session and said that she would take up the challenge today. I detailed four people as witnesses and ordered her to go ahead.'

'O.K. Is this the way to pluck? Stems and mature leaves. Supervisor, are these shoots?'

'I will get it cleaned before it is weighed,' said the *kankani*.

He looked at the weighing women. They were ready.

Their hands trembled. The indicator of the balance rose in an instant, dropped, moved a little and stopped. It was sixty-one pounds. Four pounds in excess.

Giving the sign to remove the tray, the accountant looked at the *kankani* and said, 'We cannot pay for all the sixty-one pounds. There are many flaws in the shoots.'

Letchumi was horrified. She could not believe her ears. So was the supervisor. The old man looked aghast. Letchumi called out, 'Sir,' walked fast and stood by the accountant. She pointed the index finger of her right hand at him. The skin on the sides of the finger had peeled off and the blood that had oozed out remained there congealed. She said, 'Look at this finger first before you speak. Good or bad, these fingers plucked them all. You refuse to give me weightage for my effort.'

With one look at her hand, he averted his eyes. His hands automatically took the receipt from her, noted sixty-one as the morning's weight and returned the slip of paper.

She had said that she would leave this hill if she failed to keep her pledge. But having fulfilled her promise, she did not wish to stay there any longer. It was only after she left that the accountant felt the first flush of a strong love awaken in his heart.

—Translated by Kasturi Nesaratnam

BLACK MAGIC AND NOSTALGIA

There was a five-hooded cobra in the pond of the Amman Temple. And a strange porcupine in the guava bushes near our school playground too—we were told. Besides these there was another evil spirit dwelling in the berry tree, which stood by the side of the abandoned well, not far from our playground.

We were all warned about these. Except when the teachers took the children out to the temple or to the playground, these beasts roamed about the place, our parents said, especially at noon, and they were after kiddies. The closing time of our school then was midday.

We realized little by little, when we were in grade three, the reason why the cobra, porcupine and the ghost preferred noon as their favourite time for their outing.

However, we were still afraid of the snakes found in that well. And they gave a chance to Big Vickey (there were two Vickeys with us till grade five) to prove his daring. One day, he killed a snake in the well by throwing a stone from above. From that day on, he was a hero in our eyes.

*

I can remember Ramu master smiling only once during the five long years we studied under him. Nathan was the fellow who made him smile.

Ramu master taught us English in grade four. We were doing the task of reading and forming simple sentences.

Ramu master was very particular about spelling and pronunciation. One day, he taught us three sentences:

I am a boy.
You are a girl.
This is my book.

Everyone was asked to repeat these sentences one by one.

Ours was a mixed school and so was our class. Hence, the words 'boy' and 'girl' had to be changed accordingly. When it was Nathan's turn, he happened to be looking at Leela, a big-made girl. Nathan was a tiny chap. He got up and said smartly in a loud voice, without any fear:

'I am a boy, you are my girl . . . . '

Ramu master didn't allow him to proceed. He stopped Nathan at once and started laughing.

We joined in the laughter, because we were so happy that Ramu master's facial muscles had relaxed into a smile for the first time.

*

Ramu master was the deputy head of our school. We were all afraid of his cane, which he used freely on us.

We wanted to find a way to stop this and we had a very serious discussion one day, like the forest animals in Aesop's fable, 'The Lion and the Hare'. The girls were not

A Santhan

allowed to take part in the discussion. They were so unreliable and, anyway, Ramu master rarely beat any girl.

It was Big Vickey who came up with an idea.

'We can teach him a lesson . . . .'

'What? . . .' The rest were anxious to know.

'Come closer . . . .'

We craned our necks forward and B.V. whispered:

'. . . Black magic'

'Black magic? . . .' The majority were frightened at the very words.

'A simple one . . .' B.V. assure us, 'Don't be afraid.'

And he explained the whole process.

It was vital to collect the sand from Ramu master's footprints. The sand should be roasted in an earthen pot and poured into an abandoned well—that was all. Ramu master would not be able to come to school the following day. The soles of his feet would be so badly wounded that he would not be able to walk.

B.V. said that he could get the sand roasted. The well was our responsibility. So the only task was to get the sand. It was so simple. The decision was accepted unanimously.

We were in grade four then and it was our turn to clean the school compound on Tuesdays. The girls swept the classrooms and the boys the compound.

The following Tuesday we swept the backyard first, then the sides of the compound and then at last the courtyard. It should be swept just before Ramu master's arrival. We waited. A sheet of paper was ready in B.V.'s pocket.

Ramu master arrived on time, just as we finished our sweeping. The wavy lines of the bicycle wheel marks and the foot prints of his bare feet were clearly imprinted on the white sand. B.V. collected two handfuls instead of one. Raja's ekel broom swept over the places from where sand had been removed.

As soon as school was over at midday, we all waited for the others to disperse and gathered near the hole in the boundary wall where we had kept the parcel of sand.

'Everything's ruined . . .' B.V. shouted. Only torn pieces of paper were to be seen there, on the ground.

'That dirty bird . . .' We scolded the unseen crow and waited for next Tuesday.

*

The Head Master's room was always kept locked. I had never seen him seated inside the room. His table was at the centre of the school hall, so that he could watch all the classes or all the classes could watch him.

Inside his room, there was a big almirah, a table with three legs and some benches one on top of the other. On the table, there was a beautiful picture of Saraswathi, the goddess of learning, and by its side, a slightly faded globe. On the top of the almirah, lay a world map and a map of Ceylon. There was another torn map of Ceylon hanging on the wall. Inside the almirah, there were registers, boxes of chalk etc.

We had a chance of seeing all these one day when we were asked to clean the Head Master's room.

In the backyard of the school, there were the latrines, one for the boys and the other for the girls. In front of the latrines, was a breadfruit tree with large leaves. Practically every morning, as soon as we reached school, we would run to this tree to collect the fallen leaves. Some ingenious pioneer had found that the leaf could be used to erase the writing on the slate.

When these leaves were not available, there was enough Watergrass near our drinking well. Even with these two available, the slates of several fellows smelt of saliva.

Once I was well beaten by Ramu master because of a quarrel with a fellow student over collecting breadfruit leaves.

A Santhan

*

One could go to the school from our home without passing the main road. We could go along the by-lanes, which were so lovely with their white sand. They were not metalled. During the rainy seasons these served to drain away rain water. After a heavy shower, the lanes looked much brighter and cleaner. Compounds, dense palmyrah groves and bushes of lantanna and guava alternated with one another all along the lanes. These bushes always offered us something to eat. There were guavas or lantanna fruit, if not guava shoots.

Besides these, Raja showed us one more thing. If you chewed those rounded leaves of that herb, the name of which I have forgotten, together with palmyrah shoots, your lips would get reddened like with chewing betel with areca nut, he said.

Nathan went in search of this plant and got his foot badly cut by a piece of broken glass. The blood that flowed from the wound is still fresh in my memory.

Nathan's absconding from school for a week led to Ramu master's inquiry and Raja got caught ultimately. The story ended with Raja tasting Ramu master's cane.

*

Every morning we all went together. All the little ones in our area, including Nathan, his younger brother, Raja, Siva, Easwary, Selvi . . . I had been the leader of this battalion for a long time.

As we went, the number increased. Sometimes we would go from house to house, calling out to our mates.

Kathir uncle's dog played an important role in this daily journey of ours. He was a real brute. He chased us every day all along the way—but, luckily, on the other side of the fence. Kathir uncle was a wise man. He was aware of his Veeman's ferocity and kept the gate of the compound always locked. The fence was such that there was no way Veeman could creep under it and come at us.

But our fear was constant and we tried to keep our mouths shut, while passing Kathir uncle's compound. But we could do nothing about the 'needle boxes' of the girls which made a lot of noise when they walked.

I had never seen a girl studying in our school without this box in those days. Every one of them carried an empty chocolate box, toffee box or even a talcum powder tin, with all kinds of odds and ends in it. There might be a ball of sewing thread, one or two needles, hair clips, stubs of pencils, erasers, bangles, pins, lantanna fruit and so on—all their belongings accompanied them.

There was a separate lesson for the girls needlework. At that time, we, the boys, would be engaged in handicrafts, making baskets out of neatly cut palmyrah leaves. Even after studying this craft for all those years, I couldn't manage to make a basket on my own. B.V., too, had this problem, I knew.

For the grade three promotion test, B.V. who was so bad in this subject, resorted to the assistance of Bhooshani, Nathan's big sister, who always reminded me of a pumpkin. Unfortunately, B.V. got caught by the master.

*

A music lesson was the first period for some classes each morning. Iyer master, with students around him, taught us the notes '*sa ri ga ma* . . . .' One could hear such notes even near the culvert, about a quarter of a mile away from the school. We also could hear it, during the days of late attendance and it made us think of our delay and thus of Ramu master's cane. Even now, *sa ri ga ma* makes me excited at times.

Luckily, Iyer master, realizing either his capacity or his students capacity, didn't allow this lesson to proceed beyond *sa ri ga ma*. I, too, learnt this fine art of music for two years from him, but only on the days I reached school on time.

The Head Master taught us the lesson beginning with a sentence, 'Kandasamy is a good boy . . . .' The lesson ended with a sentence '. . . children, you too should be like Kandasamy.'

The Head Master always called us 'child' or 'children'.

It was not during his period but on a Thursday, two days after our attempt to use 'Black magic' on Ramu master. It was the first period on that day. Finishing the prayers, we awaited Ramu master with our hearts beating fast.

We looked at the Head Master expectantly. We would have been happy if the Head Master had taught us English instead of Ramu master, but the Head Master hadn't come for that. He said: 'Children, be silent and do your work . . . Ramu master won't come today.' Before we could grasp what he was saying, the Head master went on, '. . . Last evening, Ramu master met with an accident. Someone's car knocked him down while he was riding home on his bicycle. Ramu master has been admitted to the hospital . . . .'

Before the Head Master could finish, we heard somebody sobbing from the back bench. We looked back. It was Big Vickey.

—*Translated by the author*

NIGHT BIRD

Though by now he had become quite inured he felt particularly torpid today. His eyes were heavy with sleep. If only he could go to bed by nine or ten like last night!

Yesterday they had not gone out because of the rain which had started in the early evening and continued through the night, his mother's voice playing accompaniment cursing the weather. What with his gnawing hunger and his mother's lamentations, he could hardly get any sleep.

Today his belly was filled to bursting and he felt very sleepy, with no prospect of getting to bed early. He was almost in tears. His legs ached with the waiting at the bus stop.

'Shall we go?' he pulled at his mother's saree.

'Shut up, you afflicted one,' she snapped, 'What will you gorge yourself with tomorrow?'

He fell silent.

A bus screeched to a halt. A lone passenger jumped out. It was not the person they were waiting for. His mother sighed with disappointment as the bus departed with a roar. The man who had got down walked off in the opposite direction. The broad road was now deserted.

Late

The street lights were widely spaced. The shutters of the lone shop behind them had been pulled down long ago. They could hear voices from within. Someone was asking the time.

'Nearing eleven,' answered another.

'Oh God. It's almost eleven.' He could hear his mother's imprecations. He knew whom she was expecting—the curly-haired man who had taken them at dusk to the corner shop and bought them snacks.

'Has the rogue deceived me? He said he would come by ten. Much chance he'll come now,' his mother grumbled.

He hoped he wouldn't come. If he turned up, who knows there they would have to wander? He was afraid he would not able to go to bed early. He prayed that the man would not come.

'God, If he doesn't come, we will go hungry tomorrow' cried his mother.

He envied his elder brother. He was the privileged one. He went wherever he pleased. If you missed him in the morning, you wouldn't see him for the rest of the day. And every morning, just to tease him, his brother would announce that he had slept well the whole night.

He had once suggested to his mother, 'Mother, take big brother with you.'

'You benighted one, your brother is too grown up. You want me to lose my livelihood?'

He didn't understand what she meant. He thought to himself. 'How can brother do so? He himself earns his livelihood during the day.' Though nobody knew where he went and what he did. His mother never saw a cent from him.

Brother was all of twelve years old, which made him four years older than him.

Old Man

'Are you really eight?' people would ask disbelievingly: he looked like a four-year-old.

Somebody was approaching in the distance. 'Is it he?' asked his mother, eagerly.

'God. Has he come, to ruin my sleep?' He squinted his eyes to see in the dark. In the dim street lights he couldn't recognize the newcomer. The figure drew nearer and he realized gratefully that it was an old man.

'It is not he.' His mother was quiet.

If only he could escape today. He was so tired. And they had walked down all the way from Eye Hospital junction. This waiting was torture.

Not that this was a new experience. And after walking about like this where did they end up? Did they go anywhere comfortable? Any old corner, rat holes . . . .

She would disappear with someone whom he did not know, leaving him outside the room or by a house, saying, 'My pet, lie down here and go to sleep. I will come and wake you when it is time.'

When she came back, he would wake up in a daze, blinking his eyes, uncertain whether he had really gone to sleep at all and where he had slept. By the time mother and son disappeared into the thinning darkness, drowsy, fatigued and spent, day would be about to break.

He would sleep through the day. During his waking moments he would feel listless and feverish, without any urge to join the other kids at play.

The first day he had asked his mother 'Where are we going?'

Was it on the first day? He could not remember. Anyway, it was one day in the beginning. His mother had replied. 'We have to meet a person I know, so come along . . . .'

No Interest

He found that it was not just one person. He was amazed at the number of people his mother knew. Though in the beginning he had been enthusiastic. He had enjoyed wandering in the brightly-lit streets of Colombo which reminded him of carnival time. He was happy getting in and out of buses holding his mother's hand.

However, as the days went by, he lost interest. He began missing his sleep. One day, when he had been exhausted like today, he had asked his mother, 'Do I have to come? Why don't you leave me and go by yourself?'

'No, my pet. Your father is not here. So you have to protect me. How can I go alone? Wouldn't the police nab me? If you are with me, nobody will ask questions . . . come,' she begged of him.

He felt sorry for her. Poor mother. And that brother of his always quarreled with her.

He really was her protector. That day when they had been waiting for the bus at Wellawatte a policeman had asked his mother so brusquely:

'What are you doing at this time of the night?'

'Waiting for the bus, boss . . . .'

'But at this hour? Don't I know what you do?'

'No boss, honestly. I came with my son to see my relative here and it became late,' she said pointing to him. The policeman had gone away and he had felt immensely proud.

He would be happy if a policeman chased them away now. He looked around. No one was in sight. He could see the clock tower of the railway station rising clearly above the other buildings.

Silent

'What is the time, mother?' he asked.
'Shut up. Do I have a watch?'
'Look . . .' he said, pointing to the clock tower.
'Eleven-thirty.'
'Shall we go? Is he coming at all?'
She made no reply.

He rested his forehead against the window-grill of the shop. The grill was cold to touch. He pressed his cheeks hard and struggled to keep his eyes open.

His mother tapped him on the back and said 'Come, we can go now . . .' He was happy. 'Shall we go? Hasn't he come?'

'May the rascal go to hell for deceiving me. We'll have nothing to eat tomorrow! Come . . . .'

He felt very sorry for his mother.

His small hand nestled in hers. She walked ahead. He pulled back and cried. 'Do we have to walk all the way home?'

'Come on. We will get a cab.'

They walked. When they reached the main road, a cab rolled up just as she had said. She clapped her hands. The driver was known to them. Cyril uncle!

'You are returning early,' Cyril uncle remarked to his mother.

'Don't ask me! Just drop us home. I will pay you later,' she replied as she opened the door of the cab and climbed in.

—Translated by A.V. Bharath

RELEASE

He was travelling in a bus.

It was the end of November. The skies hadn't opened up yet, but there had been some sporadic, good showers. Most of the fields had been sown. The breeze ruffled the shoots gently. Water in the ponds was knee-deep. Erumainakki seemed to have migrated to all the ponds and pools. Its soft flowers appeared in an unbroken stretch, as if a purple blanket had been spread on their surfaces.

The bus had stopped, it now began to inch forward again. He suddenly realized that his body and soul felt light, very soft—that he was very happy. He was surprised. How had his body and soul become so light? Was it because of the pleasant greenery of the field? The purple Erumainaki flowers? He couldn't even reason it out.

He had never experienced such a mood before. It was true that when he wrote a good story or a poem his soul felt fulfilled and ecstatic. But fulfilment and ecstasy were different from joy. Was it proper for him to conduct

Release

a lexical analysis in this way? Anyhow this lightness of body and soul was a completely different thing. He had no doubts about that. Jollity, excitement, gaiety—he had experienced them all. But this lightness was neither jollity nor excitement, it was tranquillity; a state of serenity. If needed, he could show the immaculate sky as an example of it. One could keep looking at the cloudless sky without any thoughts, without any distraction—this was how he felt!

For the past few months he had experienced an unrelieved burden within him. His workplace was in a village fourteen miles away. He opened his eyes at five o'clock, in the dawn it was that lengthy distance that appeared before his mind's eye like the Hill of Calvary. He would catch a bus or a truck before six o'clock, and midway, finishing a stream of thought as he lifted up his eyes, he would be bored to see the journey not completed yet. As he reached his destination, got off the bus and covered one and a half miles on foot, he would ask himself, 'Damn it. Why have I come at all?' It would be five by the time he reached home after finishing his job at two and boarding the bus, having foregone lunch. After that, because he gobbled his meal, the langour and heaviness of his body would torment him the whole night. When he considered that all this was because of an official's obstinacy and caprice, his burden became heavier. Carrying this heavy cross he would board the bus the next day. But why was it so soft and light today?

The bus started again from the next halt. He decided that this matter deserved deeper scrutiny. Intuitively he felt that this and whatever had happened the previous evening were linked.

It now occurred to him that though he had had a heavier meal than usual last evening after returning from his workplace, he had not felt sluggish. Soon after the meal he had read the newspaper for some time. His children—ten and eight years old—were plucking the weeds that had sprouted due to the early rains, partly as work and partly for play. He joined in their work-play. Later, when his body was dripping with sweat having chopped two or three *veera* logs for fuel, a few friends came to meet him. When he picked up the axe again, his friends having gone, some more came in; laying aside his axe, he chatted with them. As they were leaving, a friend who had come to the village just that day to spend the vacation, visited him. It was around six-thirty when he came. In less than fifteen minutes they had left for the cinema. The film finished by nine, he reached home at nine-thirty and having eaten, was with his wife till eleven-thirty; then till two o'clock he read, and then wrote a poem; then slept. Though his wife tried several times to wake him at dawn, it was only at six-forty-five that he woke. Before seven-fifteen he had washed his face, put on his clothes, finished his breakfast, and left. When he reached the bus halt at seven-thirty, he had caught this bus. Though he was very late today, neither this burden nor any other occupied his mind.

More and more passengers began to pack into the bus.

He reminded himself again of the time he had spent with his wife till half past eleven. It was a little too much for that night. Initially she hadn't liked it. Her eyelids felt heavy, she had said. But he had heaped the wood together and stoked it up. Gradually it flamed. Yes, it was very gradually that it had flamed. Her body which had been ice-cold in the rainy-season, chilled, became gradually warm. He became an expert at it. He guided her wonderfully. He plucked the strings, deeply sensitive to their notes. The music gradually became alive. The flames became more luminous. Pouring his breath on it and inhaling its scent, he made it redden into flames, he melted himself. He became one with it. The fire raged; it burst into flames. Then it was she who led him on. He beat the drums for her till she exhausted herself dancing. Both lay like children. Pulling her nightgown and the blanket which lay thrown on the ground over her, picking up his sarong and shirt, he came out into the hall. The sweat hadn't dried. He wiped himself. Coming into his study, he kindled the lamp and sat down.

When his friend had insisted on going to the cinema last evening, he had hesitated. He had agreed to write a poem for the tree planting ceremony to be held the next day by the institution he was working for. It had to be a long poem. To compose that could take one or two hours. He had feared that if he went to the cinema he might run short of time. But with the brash courage that he could complete the poem after returning from the cinema, he had left. The thought of the poem had pricked him even when he was with his wife. He usually fell asleep with her. Now, when he sat in his study, his thoughts were focused on the poem. Before he started, however, Hema Malini's eyes from the pages of the *Illustrated Weekly* had caught his attention. He couldn't prevent himself from reading about her. 'Perhaps there were other companions to luck, like hard work and persistence, a sense of dignity for this work, and the consciousness of the importance of doing that job with earnestness and diligence.' He underlined those lines of her statement with a black ball-point pen. Respecting her for those lines, he finished writing the long poem.

The bus stopped at a halt again. Shrinking from the breeze blowing through the green fields that struck his face and the gust that untidied his 'hippie' hair style he muttered a few lines of the poem from memory:

'We have often greeted the Spring
We have enjoyed the fertile Spring

You are the daughter of Spring—bloom
You are the heart of Spring's growth
To greet you we assemble, O Tree
To grow you we've come, dear Tree.'

The bus started again. Suddenly a thought flashed across his mind.

'I've been busy the whole of yesterday . . . .'

So the secret was his 'being busy', was it? Being involved? But then he saw it differently. Though he had done some work, he had not thought much of that. He hadn't forsaken the Cinema for Poetry. He hadn't forsaken Love for Poetry. He hadn't closed his eyes to Hema Malini for Poetry. He hadn't spoilt his sleep for the sake of the bus. Even now he wasn't worried about reaching in time. So that solved it? Hmm . . . ? But he was still not satisfied.

For goodness sake, give up. Why should he worry himself to find an explanation for that. He was not willing now to burden his mind.

In an indifferent mood he mumbled the lines of the poem again. 'You are the daughter of Spring's bloom, You are the heart of Spring's growth . . . .'

He watched the marutha trees which ran along both sides of the long stretch and disappeared. He watched flocks of small black birds perching on the telegraph wires that ran along the edges of the fields, flying away and then perching again on the wires. The bus was still running.

—Translated by Suresh Canagarajah

NOTES ON THE AUTHORS

Writers in English

Akeemana, Gamini : a journalist and a writer whose stories have appeared in local journals and anthologies; a playwright too.

Fernando, Chitra : author of several collections of stories for children and three collections for adults, *Three Women* (1983), *Between Worlds* (1988), *Women There and Here: Progressions in Six Stories* (1994).

Fernando, Vijita : a journalist, a writer in both English and Sinhalese, and also a well-known translator.

Lokuge, Chandani : author of *Moth and Other Stories* (1992).

Mohideen, Rehana : a contributor of stories to local journals.

Ranasinghe, Anne : better known as a poet, she has published stories in *With Words We Write Our Lives Past Present Future* (1972) and *Desire and Other Stories* (1994); a contributor to *Short Story International*.

Goonewardene, James : author of *The Third Woman* (1963), *The Rebel* (1979), *Yukti and Other Stories* (1991), *To Follow the Sun* (1995), collections of short stories; *The Waiting Earth* (1966) and *Amulet* (1994), novels. *Giraya* (1971), a novella; and a kind of memoir, *A Way of Life* (1987).

Writers in Sinhalese

Amarasekara, Gunadasa : critic, poet and novelist; his early work shows the influence of Western writers and forms but he now looks more to native sources for inspiration.

Balasuriya, Somaratne : author of *Vap Magul* (1987), a novel, and *The Cart* (1992), a collection of short stories; editor of *Vimansa*.

Sarachchandra, Ediriwira, : critic and playwright in Sinhalese; novelist in both English and Sinhalese; winner of the Asan World Prize in 1983 and the Ramon Magsaysay Award in 1988.

Wickremasinghe, Martin : journalist, essayist, novelist and critic, his literary career spans a period of over half a century; he is the founder of the modern Sinhalese novel.

Writers in Tamil

Ramaiah, N.S.M. : the foremost short story writer among the plantation Tamils; his first collection, *A Basketful of*

Tea Leaves, appeared in 1980; he has also written radio plays.

Santhan, A. : author of seven collections of short stories, a novel and a travelogue in Tamil; and a collection of stories in English, *The Sparks* (1990).

Sivalingam, Shanmugam : a contributor of stories to the newspapers.

NOTES ON THE TRANSLATORS

Bharath, A.V. : bio-data not available

Canagarajah, Suresh : Senior Lecturer in English, University of Jaffna, he has contributed poems to local journals.

Dharmapriya, A.T. : formerly Lecturer in English at Teachers' and Technical Colleges, later Additional Director and Head of ESP Programme, Ministry of Higher Education, he is presently English Language Consultant to the Secondary Education Development Project funded by the Asian Development Bank. He has contributed poems to local journals and ELT articles to journals abroad.

Nesaratnam, Kasturi : formerly a teacher at Holy Family Convent, Colombo, she is presently co-editor of *Sai Marg*, a quarterly journal in English published by the Sai Organisation of Sri Lanka.

Obeyesekere, Ranjini : a translator of Sinhalese folk-verse, poetry and fiction, her translation of the 13th-century *Saddharmaratnavaliya* as *Jewels of the Doctrine* was published by the State University of New York Press in 1991.

Siriwardena, Reggie : critic, poet and playwright, he brought out his first collection of translations from the Russian, French and Spanish, *Many Voices*, in 1975, and later translations of two plays of Alexander Pushkin, *The Covetous Knight* and *The Stone Guest* in 1970. He has also published translations of the poems of Anna Akhmatova and Marina Tsvetaeva; collections of original poems, *Waiting for the Soldier* (1989), *To the Muse of Insomnia* (1990); and collections of his own plays, *The Almsgiving and Other Plays* (1994), and *Octet* (1995).

Glossary

akke	elder sister
aiya	elder brother
Bana Potha	Buddhist religious book
bo tree	the tree under which Buddha attained enlightenment; sacred to Buddhists
Dinamina	a Sinhalese newspaper
kadalay	gram
Kalathoni	Illicit immigrant
kevun	Sinhalese sweetmeats made of rice flour and honey
kiri bhuth	milk rice
kokis	Sinhalese version of Dutch kockjes (cookies), crisp sweetmeats
lakka	A kind of broadcloth from the Dutch, laken.
machchang	pal
miris kudu	chilli powder
nangi	younger sister
suddhas	whites
thaththa	father
vaha	the evil eye